P9-DFQ-957

BIG MIKE HENEY

Irish Prince of the Iron Rails

Builder of the White Pass and Yukon and
Copper River Northwestern Railways

OLD
#50

Elizabeth A. Tower

PO Box 221974 Anchorage, Alaska 99522-1974

ISBN 1-59433-010-7

Library of Congress Catalog Card Number: 2003098684

Copyright 2003 by Elizabeth A. Tower
—Second Edition—
—Third Printing 2005—

All rights reserved, including the right of
reproduction in any form, or by any mechanical
or electronic means including photocopying or
recording, or by any information storage or
retrieval system, in whole or in part in any
form, and in any case not without the
written permission of the author and publisher.

Dedication

Big Mike Heney, Irish Prince of the Iron Rails, is dedicated to Samuel Graves, Dr Fenton Whiting, and Rex Beach who made the "Irish Prince" live for future generations.

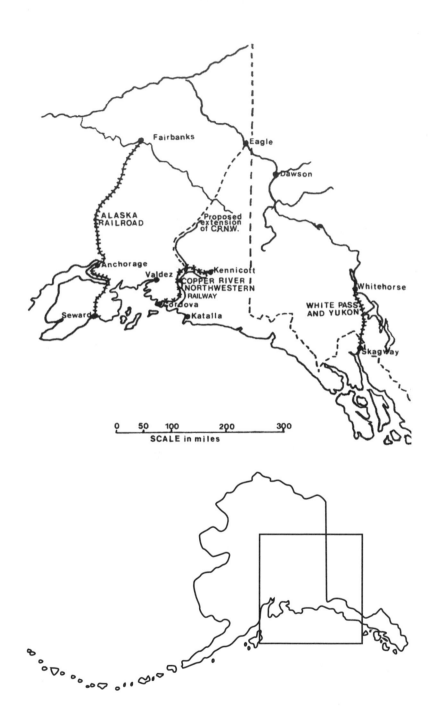

Fairbanks

Eagle

Dawson

ALASKA
RAILROAD

Proposed
extension
of C.R.N.W.

Anchorage

Kennicott

Valdez

COPPER RIVER
NORTHWESTERN
RAILWAY

Whitehorse

Cordova

WHITE PASS
AND YUKON

Seward

Katalla

Skagway

```
0    50   100        200        300
SCALE in miles
```

Contents

Michael James Heney, "The Irish Prince." 1864-1910
Courtesy of Roy Minter collection

PROLOGUE
"THE BOY CONTRACTOR"

Nature richly endowed Michael James Heney for the times in which he lived. Known as "Big Mike" to his railroad crews in Washington, Canada and Alaska, he was at home in frontline construction tents. In the financial and social circles of Seattle, San Francisco, New York and London he was called the "Irish Prince." To his many friends he was simply "M.J."

Mike Heney had those qualities that assured success on the western frontier at the turn of the century. Vision of the future prompted him to undertake projects shunned by less daring men. Although he lived only 45 years, he founded a city, amassed a fortune and inspired a best selling novel. Without technical training, he built two railroads considered impossible by the leading engineers of his day. A ready Irish smile drew people to him and they became his friends for life. Wherever Big Mike led, his workers followed; each proud to be one of Heney's men.

As gold lured men westward, railroads followed. Rail building fascinated Mike Heney, the son of an Irish immigrant farmer. As a boy of fourteen, he ran away from his Pembroke, Ontario home to work on the Canadian Pacific Railroad. School did not interest young Heney. His idol was his uncle John, an energetic Ottawa merchant, entrepreneur and construction contractor. Mike moved west with the railroad, driving mules and laying rails. In March 1883, he joined the survey crew of John Stevens, the engineer who charted a path for the railway through the Selkirk mountains. While working on the right-of-way down the Fraser River in British

Columbia, he learned to measure grades, blast cliffs, build tunnels and estimate costs. His greatest natural talent was his ability to inspire working men. By the time Lord Strathcona drove the last spike on the Canadian Pacific in 1885, Heney, though barely 21 years old, was already established as a railroad contractor.

Heney remained in British Columbia for several years upgrading and revising tracks on the Canadian Pacific. In 1887 he was hired to construct a 40 mile section of the Seattle, Lake Shore and Eastern Railroad between Sedro-Woolley and Sumas. He moved permanently to Seattle, where he was known as the "boy contractor." Other railroad jobs in Western Washington followed, including a spur of the Northern Pacific beyond Everett.

Alaska beckoned Heney in 1897. He took a contract to build an hydraulic line on the Kenai Peninsula for the Anchor Point Gold Mining Company. The work consisted of digging a ditch to carry water from an inland lake on top of a high bluff, so the lake water under high pressure could be used to wash down small amounts of gold from the beach sands. This small mining operation was soon forgotten, but Heney developed a lifelong fascination for Alaska.

The Anchor Point job taught Big Mike valuable lessons about transporting a labor force to a far distant construction site. One episode nearly cost him his life! The story is told in the July 10, 1897 issue of the Sitka *Alaskan*:

> In the midst of the baseball game that followed the races, pistol shots were heard in the Millmore house and a large man with a pistol in his hand was seen to run out and make for the wilds back of town. Everybody flocked to the Millmore house and learned that two men had been shot, John Rice and Michael Heney. The men were strangers in the city having just arrived from the Westward where they had been doing contract work for the Anchor Point Gold Mining Co., and the man that did the shooting was John Zdenek, an employee and also a stranger here. The Anchor Point Co. immediately offered a reward for the capture of Zdenek.

Marshal Williams at once went to the Indian Ranch and started his Indian Policemen, Jackson, Bean and Rudolph in pursuit. Gathering a few trusty associates together these Indians started on the trail and in less than two hours had captured their man in the bushes back of Swan Lake.

This quick capture of the man was a genuine surprise to tourists and many of them expressed the opinion that detectives in the east should come here and take lessons from the red man.

After the man was captured and safely caged, people began to ask what was the nature of the wounds and what was the cause of the shooting! As near as could be ascertained it was as follows.

Early last spring The Anchor Point Mining Co. gave Michael Heney a contract to put a six mile ditch through their placers. Heney engaged a large force of men in Seattle, John Zdenek being among the number, and agreed to give them transportation to Anchor Point and return and pay them 30 cents per hour while working on said ditch. At the close of the contract, Heney chartered a sailing vessel from the Pacific Steam Whaling Co. to send the workmen back to Seattle, but the men refused to go on the vessel thinking it to be unsafe. Heney claimed then that he was under no obligation to them, but finally entered into an agreement with them to pay their transportation to Juneau. In accordance with this agreement all hands came to Sitka on the last *Dora* and had to wait here for the *Topeka*.

Zdenek was among the number who stopped at the Millmore house and when Mr. Millmore passed around collecting board bills Zdenek told him that contractor Heney would pay his three dollars.

Mr. Heney promptly refused to pay any other than his own individual bill. Zdenek told him he had better pay it, and on his still refusing Zdenek went out. In a short time he came back, opened the door and fired first at John Rice who was sitting alongside of and talking to Heney, and then shot at Heney. He

9

shot to kill for evidently both shots were aimed at the heart.

A large book in the breast pocket of Rice and bad aim at Heney only prevented the wounds from being fatal. Dr. Rogers dressed the wounds and the men were able to take their departure.

Alaska was soon to see more of Michael J. Heney, but on his future contracts, Big Mike preferred to hire locally whenever possible.

SKAGWAY
"WAIT PATIENTLY AND YOU'LL RIDE"

$\mathbf{M}$ike Heney and his men arrived back in Seattle from the Cook Inlet job just in time to greet the *Portland* when it arrived on July 17, 1897 with news of the Klondike gold strike. Prospectors aboard showed nuggets that dwarfed the meager returns from Anchor Point beach sands.

A miner named Bob Henderson was the first to find gold on Gold Bottom Creek. He invited George Washington Carmacks to join him, but Carmacks preferred to prospect on his own with his two Indian companions Skookum Jim and Tagish Charlie. Their finds, in the summer of 1896, along Rabbit Creek were even richer. Carmacks passed the word on to other prospectors and the Klondike Gold Rush was on. Prospectors waited until the Yukon River was free of ice in the late spring of 1897 to return by boat to San Francisco and Seattle. An estimated 5000 stampeders and 3000 horses flooded the passes into the Klondike the following fall.

Heney was convinced that better access to the Yukon River drainage was needed. While recovering from the arm wound received in Sitka, he questioned men returning from the Klondike. He studied all the material he could find about trails through the coastal mountains. Two passes at the head of Lynn Canal provided the shortest routes to the Yukon headwater lakes. Local Indians used the rugged Chilkoot Pass to go from Dyea to Lake Bennett. Although it was the shortest, it had a section, known as "the Scales" that was too steep and rocky for wagons and pack animals. Stampeders eventually designed an aerial tramway to carry supplies over this sheer wall of ice and rock.

The White Pass, discovered in 1888 by Capt. William Moore and named for Sir Thomas White, Canadian Minister of Interior, ran 25 miles north along the Skagway River. It was 10 miles longer than the Chilkoot Pass, but 600 feet lower and wide enough for horses and wagons. During the winter of 1898, George Brackett, ex-mayor of Minneapolis, spent $185,000 to build a wagon road to the summit. The road had a series of steep climbs, zigzagging wildly along the sheer cliffs. At Devil's Hill, the slate was slippery and the trail only two feet wide. Many pack horse slipped and fell, or were pushed, into the canyon below, giving it the name "Dead Horse Gulch."

Canada and the United States were still disputing the boundary at the head of Lynn Canal, both claiming land at the entrance to the White Pass where Captain Moore had established the town of Skagway. Uncertainty about this boundary prompted the Canadian government to consider helping William Mackenzie and Donald Mann build an all Canadian railroad up the Stikine River to Teslin Lake.

Heney had no hope of help from the government for the railroad he hoped to build. He borrowed money and booked passage with his friend, Captain Johnny O'Brien, on the *Utopia*, landing in Skagway on March 31, 1898. Heney shouldered his pack and set out to see for himself the country he had been studying. After looking at the Chilkoot Pass, he was convinced that a railroad could not climb the Scales. He was even more certain on April 3 when a massive avalanche buried prospectors preparing to cross the Chilkoot. Heney identified many construction problems that he would have to face in building a railroad through the White Pass, but was convinced that he was the man to do it. The lack of financial backing was the next problem he would have to face.

After several weeks on the trail, Heney returned on April 21 to Skagway and checked in at the St. James Hotel. He was exhausted and covered with dirt, having walked the entire 40 miles from Lake Bennett that day. Fate was on his side. The very men with the solution to his funding problem happened to be guests at the St. James Hotel that night.

The Close Brothers, a London banking firm, had hired Sir Thomas Tancrede, a British engineer, and Erastus C. Hawkins from Seattle, to assess whether a railroad could be built through the White Pass. Tancrede and Hawkins, along with John Hislop, Hawkins' assistant, had met in the St. James Hotel bar each night for two weeks to discuss their findings. Tancrede, whose opinion the Close Brothers were relying upon, had difficulty visualizing a railroad line through the splintered rock walls and jagged spurs of granite half buried in ice and snow. The men were almost ready to send a negative report to London when Hawkins spied Heney checking in. The desk clerk informed Hawkins that this new arrival was also studying the possibility of a railroad, and Hawkins invited Heney to join the group. In spite of fatigue, Big Mike agreed to come down as soon as he cleaned up.

The Close Brothers became interested in the distant Yukon when they acquired by default franchises to build a railroad through the White Pass. Back in 1895, Captain Moore convinced Ernest Billinghurst, an English civil engineer, that such a road could be built. Billinghurst presented the idea to Charles Herbert Wilkinson, who was looking over investment opportunities for himself and his British associates. Although there was not yet enough traffic to the Yukon headwaters to justify a railroad, Wilkinson had the foresight to obtain charters from the United States, Canada and British Columbia. His employers rejected his railway proposal, but let him keep the charters, providing he paid them 10,000 pounds in January 1898 and 20,000 pounds the following May. Wilkinson borrowed the 10,000 pounds from William Brooks Close. When he was unable to raise the additional money, the Close Brothers acquired his charter to build a railroad in an unfamiliar area halfway around the world.

Heney joined the men in the St. James Hotel bar, and their discussions continued throughout the night. Heney described in detail the route he would recommend, including the nearly perpendicular rock wall at mile 15 that would require a tunnel. Big Mike's knowledge and enthusiasm soon overcame Sir Thomas' doubts. That night they decided to build the White Pass and Yukon Railway, pending approval by the Close Brothers. Tancrede, Hawkins, and Heney left Skagway the following morning on the *Rosalie* leaving Hislop to continue surveying. On the three day trip to Seattle, they estimated the costs of construction. To save money, they decided to use a narrow gauge, with three feet between rails, rather than standard gauge, where the rails are more than four feet apart. They would only need to cut a ten foot road bed in the sheer rock faces.

Since the railroad would need connections in Seattle to buy and ship construction supplies to Skagway, Heney contacted his brother in Canada and persuaded him to take charge of that part of the business. Shortly after the *Rosalie* arrived back in port, Michael James and Patrick Augustus Heney formed Seattle Sand and Gravel.

William Brooks Close in London approved of the plan, but advised proceeding with caution. The outcome of the Spanish- American War was in doubt, and he was uncertain how the laws of the United States would apply to the District of Alaska. On May 14, 1898, Congress extended provisions of the Homestead Act to Alaska, making it possible to grant right-of-way, station acreage and materials, such as timber and stone, for building a railroad. London gave full approval and established the Pacific and Arctic Railway and Navigation Company to file the Alaska part of the survey under provisions of this Act. This new Alaskan company was combined with the British Columbia Yukon Railway Company and the British Yukon Railway Company to form the White Pass and Yukon Company, a Canadian corporation, with Samuel Graves as president. E.C. Hawkins would be chief engineer and John Hislop assistant engineer and chief surveyor. They hired Heney as "labor contractor", to receive a five percent commission on wages paid to laborers engaged in the actual construction of the railroad. Workers would be paid 30 cents an hour for a 10 hour day, less one dollar a day for board, consisting of a bunk and three meals.

Late in the afternoon of May 27, 1898, the *City of Seattle* and the *Utopia* reached Skagway with the first cargo of building material and a work force of 100 men. Heney brought some key men with him from Seattle, but hoped to hire most of his laborers from among the hoards of gold-seekers in Skagway.

Fenton B. Whiting, the railroad doctor, wrote of his first impressions of the new town in *Grit. Grief and Gold*:

> Skagway, composed mainly of saloons, dance halls and hotels of the frontier type, loomed in all her glory. In the saloons long, crude bars decorated the side walls, lined with dozens of thirsty souls from all walks of life and nations. Here the millionaire rubbed elbows with the veriest roughneck, the dance hall girl, the soldier, the mounted police and the U.S. Marshal...
>
> Stalwart, sober men paced the streets and mingled with the drunken herd, and dreamed of the day they would return to loved ones in the States with the gold which the Yukon promised them. Hundreds of men from all walks of life, lawyers doctors, college breds, common laborers, "remittance men" from the old country, out West for the peace of mind and health of wealthy and aristocratic relatives over the Atlantic; even the nobility was represented here by worthless counts and no-accounts, mostly the latter, many already stranded, others waiting for the trail to open to go on inside with their outfits over the strenuous journey through the "Pass", others looking for work of any kind. These latter idle men proved a great boon to the new railroad enterprise looking for men in all capacities, from the lowest to the highest. No young city ever boasted a greater variety of humanity and notables.

Dr. Whiting, himself, benefited from having such a diverse group of employees. Called upon to perform emergency surgery, he summoned a doctor, whom he had identified on one of the crews, to assist at the operation. After the surgery was completed, the doctor resumed his work with pick and shovel.

Aspiring gold seekers did not always provide a reliable labor force. In the words of Camp-foreman Hugh Foy, "There was always some a-coming, and some a-going, and some working." Samuel Graves described one of the most serious incidents in his book, *On The White Pass Payroll*:

> By August 8th, 1898, we had got our working force

up to a little over 2000 men. On that day the news came of the new gold discovery in Atlin, comparatively near our line, and the excitement spread like wild fire through our camps. Our men left in droves, most of them without waiting to draw their pay, but on the other hand most of them took with them our picks and shovels. In 48 hours our working force was reduced to below 700 men and it was October before we were able to fill up our ranks again.

The Atlin desertion was doubly serious since Heney had to send an emergency order to his brother in Seattle for more picks and shovels, costing $16 apiece.

The Spanish American War was still in progress, creating other supply problems. Ships in Seattle were being used to support the war effort, so Heney had to renovate several wrecked sailing ships for use as supply barges.

A right-of-way problem delayed the start of construction for several weeks after the men and materials arrived. The area on the east bluff, where the railroad planned to lay track, was occupied by squatters. Hawkins wanted the City Council to grant temporary permission to run trains down Broadway, the main street in town, until title to the land on the east bluff could be cleared. Broadway merchants objected to the plan, and the problem remained unsolved for several weeks while supplies piled up on the docks. After two inconclusive town meetings, the railroad management gave its ultimatum. The City Council adjourned late on the night of June 15, stating that they would give permission the next morning. Most of the councilmen slept late. When they awoke the next morning, they saw 200 men busy laying tracks down the center of Broadway. Big Mike had gone ahead, permit or no permit. Eventually the railroad was able to purchase land on the east bluff. There were soon two tracks set in Skagway; passenger trains continuing to run on Broadway.

The railroad had to contend with total lack of law and order in Skagway. Jefferson Randolph "Soapy" Smith came to town in late 1897, and ruled a gang of 300 gamblers, thugs and pickpockets, called "the lambs." Members of Soapy's gang preyed on the gold-seekers by setting up drinking and gambling tents along the trails. Samuel Graves describes what happened when they tried to interfere with railroad construction:

> Heney's rule about liquor was strict and simple -
> "No liquor allowed in camp" When Camp 3 (Rocky
> Point) was started, one of Soapy Smith's gang set up
> a gambling and drinking tent near by. Heney ordered
> him off. He refused to move his tent and said he
> "guessed it had as good a right to be there as Heney's"
> which was true, of course. But Heney was not the

Clearing right of way on Broadway. June 1898
Anchorage Museum of History and Art

man to split straws over nice questions of technical rights. He sent for Foy, the camp foreman, and pointing to a big rock just above the drinking den, he told Foy in the hearing of the owner, "That rock has got to be out of there by 5 tomorrow morning - not a minute later, mind" Then he walked off, and told Soapy's friend to think it over. He evidently concluded that it was a bluff and went to bed with an easy mind.

Next morning early Foy sent a rock gang to put a few sticks of dynamite in the rock. They reported "all ready" at ten minutes to five. At five minutes to five he sent a man to the tent to wake its occupant. He refused with bad language to get up so early. Then Foy went himself and said, "In one minute by this watch I will give the order to touch off the fuse.

17

It will burn for one minute and then that rock will arrive here or hereabouts The man in bed told Foy to go to Hades. Foy replied, "I'm too busy to go this morning but you will unless you jump lively - Fire!'- Then he used the 60 seconds left to retire in good order behind a sheltering point of rock, where he was joined ten seconds later by the tent owner in his underwear (it is another custom of the country to sleep in them), and together they witnessed the

White Pass and Yukon Railway builders: left to right, Hugh Foy, Dr, Whiting, Heney, Hawkins, Samuel Graves, and Hislop.
Yukon Archives, Whitehorse

blast and total destruction of the tent and its stock of liquors. Then Foy went up to Heney's tent and reported, "That rock is down, sir."

"Where is the man?" asked Heney.

"The last I saw of him he was going down the trail in his underclothes, cursing."

"That's all right," said Heney, and we had no more bother with that sort.

Samuel Graves arrived in Skagway on July 2, 1898. He declined an invitation from Soapy Smith to join him at the head July 4th parade. Two days later, he and his "Three IIs," Hawkins, Hislop and Heney, attended a citizen meeting, called to protest the robbing of a young Australian prospector by the

The first locomotive in Alaska: Skagway, July, 20 1898.
Deadman's Photo, Skagway

Tourists comfortably seated on flat cars.
Deadman's Photo, Skagway

Smith gang. The citizens anticipated fighting. They sent Heney and Hawkins to the pass to prevent the escape of gang members. Heney and Dr. Whiting were relaxing in a tent at Rocky Point when they got word that Soapy and Frank Reid had been shot. Dr. Whiting returned to Skagway where he operated on Reid and did an autopsy on Soapy Smith. For the next few days, Big Mike and his men collected "lambs" as they tried to escape through the pass.

Although the people in Skagway referred to their new railway as the "Wait Patiently and You'll Ride", the Three Hs knew that Klondike stampeders were not patient. They didn't want to make anyone wait longer than was absolutely necessary. As soon as tracks were laid, trains moved. The first passenger train ran a distance of six miles out of Skagway on

Heney, Hawkins, and Dr. Whiting greet excursion passengers at Porcupine Point. August 23, 1898
Yukon Archives, Whitehorse

July 21, 1898. The July 23rd edition of *The Daily Alaskan* carried the headline, "Summer Tourists Come To Skagway they Ride Up the Railroad and are Enchanted." The article further described that 150 people were "comfortably seated" on temporary seats on three box cars. The train steamed up Broadway with its passengers, which included Skagway residents, Yukoners and even some tourists. Then it crossed the newly constructed trestle to the west side of the Skagway River. Along the right-of-way, crews were refining the grade, clearing the rock cuts, constructing retaining walls, aligning the track, and hauling materials to the construction front. The train inched across a partially completed bridge over the East Fork of the Skagway River, and started climbing towards the summit. Suddenly the whistle blew and the train stopped in front of a large perpendicular cliff. They were at Rocky Point where the tracks ended. After Heney showed them the work at Rocky Point, the guests toured Dr. Whiting's hospital and had lunch. The hearty meal, graced with such luxuries as

Tourists train above Pitchfork Falls.
Yukon Archives, Whitehorse

chutney and caviar, was the first of many banquets hosted by Contractor Heney during the construction of his railroads.

There were no more free excursions. By the first of August people were paying several dollars for their rides to Rocky Point. The railroad was soon earning its keep by hauling miners and supplies to the end of the tracks. Brackett's haul road was both a blessing and a curse to the railroad builders. Although it competed with the railway for the freight-hauling dollar, Heney had to keep it open for moving supplies. Since

21

rock from blasting on the right-of-way cuts above the haul road frequently threatened to close it, railroad workers were forced to spend almost as much time in clearing debris from Brackett's Road as they did in building the railroad. Keeping Brackett's Road open was only one of many problems ahead for Big Mike and his men as they pushed on to the summit of the White Pass.

While working 18 hours a day and punching ahead relentlessly, Heney still proved himself a pleasant man to work with, as expressed in an anonymous verse found in the papers of John Hislop:

> There's our friend, Mr. Heney, who's probably as brainy
> As any in Skagway, I think,
> Whose bright pleasant smile shortens many a mile
> As he hands you his flask with a wink.

Near Rocky Point: back row, Foy, Hawkins, Hislop, and Heney. September 18, 1898
Yukon Archives, Whitehorse

ON TO THE SUMMIT
A BANQUET AT TWENTY BELOW

Heney was everywhere along the right-of-way, supervising all phases of construction. He soon had eight work camps in full operation between Skagway and the summit. Two shifts of men worked

Graves, Hislop, Hawkins, Heney with dogs.
Yukon Archives, Whitehorse

ten hours, day and night, so Heney was often on the trail for eighteen hours at a time. He usually traveled on horseback, accompanied by two large dogs. A cot was available for him in each camp in case he needed a few hours sleep. He enforced rigid rules forbidding alcohol and smoking on the job although he was a heavy smoker and a connoisseur of fine liquor, with a supply of whisky and imported wine always on hand. Big Mike's growing influence along the right-of-way far outstripped his authority as labor contractor .

When construction crews approached the White Pass Summit, which was unofficially considered the Canadian boundary, they were stopped by the Northwest Mounted Police. Although the White Pass and Yukon Company was a Canadian corporation, they did not have permission to enter Canada Dr. Whiting recounts how Heney engaged the colorful William Robinson as "unofficial Ambassador to British Columbia" Robinson was known as "Stikine Bill" because he had worked

Turning the first Canadian soil. October 4, 1898
Yukon Archives, Whitehorse

previously on the all Canadian route along the Stikine river. The Mackenzie-Mann railroad plan had failed and many workers, like Robinson, had come to work for Heney. Stikine Bill, an immense man weighing over 300 pounds, was a native of North Anson, Maine, with a wry sense of humor and picturesque style of speech. His diplomatic portfolio consisted of two bottles of whisky and two boxes of cigars, with which to celebrate the birthday of the officer in charge of the summit mountie post. Robinson returned the next evening and reported that the "treaty had been signed" early that same morning after they had killed the last bottle. He also reported;

"Ain't no boundary line there now. We fought over all the old battles again - Zulus, Egypt and India - he's been in all uv'em, and I'll bet I'm the best drilled man in Alaska right now in military tic-tacks; it's all I've heard all day."

An informal ceremony was held October 4,1898 to mark the entry into what was commonly referred to as "British Territory." In order to reach the site of the ceremony in a meadow five miles beyond the summit, invited dignitaries rode the train to the end of the tracks at Heney Station, where they were met by Heney and Hislop. They were escorted to Dr. Whiting's hospital tent, where they received spirits to fortify them for a four mile horseback ride to White Pass City. At Summit Lake, boatmen in Peterborough canoes paddled them four and a half miles to the north end of the lake. Then they walked another half mile, finally reaching their destination at four thirty that afternoon. *The Victoria Daily Colonist* on October 12th reported that, following the ceremony, the guests and railway officials went to a specially erected dining tent, where several bottles of Pommery and Four Crown Scotch were downed. Following a sumptuous feast, the guests thanked the railway by singing *For They Are Jolly Good Fellows.* Some of the guests, enroute to Dawson City, continued down Fraser Lake to Log Cabin by canoe. Other guests returned with Heney and Hislop on horseback, spending the night at White Pass City and returning to Skagway the following day.

The day after the sod-turning ceremony, both Summit and Fraser lakes were glazed with ice, and the ground was frozen solid. Soon a violent storm brought five inches of snow. Some days the weather was so severe that little could be accomplished at the most difficult section of the right-of-way south of the actual summit. Crews had started work during the summer on the sixty-degree slope of Slippery Rock, a huge slab of granite projecting from the face of Tunnel Mountain, by suspending men on ropes and lowering them to the grade site. Beyond Slippery Rock, an enormous rock face led to a 150 foot chasm on the other side of which was a sheer granite buttress. The builder's task was to drive a tunnel into the eastern wall of the buttress and bridge the 150 foot void. The chasm could not be bridged until tracks were laid so trains could haul the heavy bridging equipment.

Another obstacle for Heney to overcome was a canyon at Mile 19 that was too wide and deep to cross with an ordinary trestle or timber span. To avoid months of delay while waiting to erect a metal cantilever bridge, Heney's men built a switchback to move trains from one side of the canyon to the other. They laid tracks on both sides of the canyon with a turntable to turn the trains around.

Big Mike was in his element. No one could doubt his ability to drive men, beasts and machines to the limit of their endurance. Hawkins was occupied with political, financial and legal affairs, leaving Heney effectively in charge of all construction details. Laborers were easier to find during the winter because they were anxious to earn a grubstake for the next summer. By the end of January, Heney had 1800 men working, half of them shoveling snow. Crews finished blasting the tunnel on January 29, 1899. Early in February, they bridged the chasm.

When not otherwise occupied, Heney joined Hislop on surveying expeditions, covering great distances on snowshoes. Early in the construction, the London firm that acted as trustee for the railway shareholders, retained Canadian civil engineer, Robert Brydone-Jack, to see that work was done in accordance with the contract. Although Samuel Graves feared that the "three Hs" would resent this intrusion. Heney and Hislop readily accepted Brydone-Jack as a co-worker, and Graves was able to report:

> As the winter progressed the sympathy between the three men living and working and sharing dangers and hardships in common became deeper and deeper till they were more united than most brothers.
>
> But there was one moot point that never was settled. Heney and Hislop were like mountain goats upon a trail. Long before Jack's advent they had "tried one another out" in many a terrible day's climbing and covering ground, until each had admitted to himself that the other was his equal on the trail. Then Jack came to live with them and because he was as a brother to them they watched his performance on the trail with affectionate interest. Now Jack was physically a magnificent man, and his pluck was

unsurpassed, and moreover, it so happened that he rather prided himself in never having met a man who could "stay with him" on the trail. Any man who bumped up against either Heney or Hislop in such a mood was likely to meet with trouble.

But for a long time they had no suspicion of it,

Hislop and Heney snowshoeing on the White Pass Summit.
Yukon Archives, Whitehorse

and merely thought he did very well indeed. Of course no word was spoken between them of all this, but gradually it dawned on Heney and Hislop that Jack, whose performance they had been watching with pride and interest, was in reality "going jealous" of them and anxious in the perfectly friendly way to establish his supremacy on the trail. This state of affairs could not last. Without a word said - all felt that the question had to be settled when they started on their last trail together in this world, one morning early in February 1899.

The snow was deep, the trail was heavy, the cold was bitter, the wind on the summit of the Pass was fierce, almost preventing progress at times. Part of the time there was a blizzard, and at all times the trail was steep. Jack had never seen Heney and Hislop in real earnest before nor ever come across their like. Few men could have stayed with them that day till noon when they halted for food and rest. Jack however was one of the few. But he had not been hardened to fast work on the trail as they had for many months previously, and his exertions had begun to tell on even his magnificent physical powers when they "hit the trail" again after the brief noon interval. He was now on the defensive and doggedly he stuck to it all afternoon in the failing light and through the increasing cold.

In vain they urged him to "take it easy"- the more they protested, the more he persisted, with failing strength but unfaltering determination not to give in. When they reached camp at dark, Jack was exhausted and never knew that his generous friends were any less so. It was a bitter night, the thermometer far below zero, and the tent gave little protection from the fierce wind to the exhausted man. The morning found him enfeebled, unrested, and feverish. But he scorned the idea of going down to our Hospital at Skagway. Some days passed in camp, in miserable anxiety by Heney and Hislop, and increasing fever on Jack's part. Then came the day when they carried him in his blankets to the engine of the "work train" and uncoupled her to run down to Skagway. Pneumonia had set in.

In spite of a hair-raising run down to the hospital, Brydone-Jack died the following day. For months Heney and Hislop mourned. The trustees in London showed their confidence in the "three Hs" by appointing Hawkins to be their agent.

On February 20, the first passenger train, with 100 invited guests, reached White Pass Summit. A banner headline in The *Daily Alaskan* proclaimed it "The Proudest Day in Alaska History." The editor described the occasion as "a sumptuous banquet on a snowcapped granite wall, two thousand nine hundred feet above the sea, with an Italian blue sky over head and brilliant sunshine illuminating miles and miles of sparkling snow,

**First passenger train on the summit
of White Pass. February 20, 1899**
Yukon Archives, Whitehorse

and the temperature -22 degrees." Hugh Foy greeted the guests and directed them to two tents - one with a blazing heater and decanters of sherry for the ladies, the other stocked with cigars and hard liquor for the men. Guests were then escorted to the dining tent where they were served a lavish meal that included caviar and champagne. Heney gave an after-lunch speech, describing the difficulties and dangers his men faced in pushing the railway to the summit. The Reverend Mr. Sinclair then spoke highly of Heney, mentioning the many kindnesses he had seen him perform both in business and private life.

The jovial tone ceased when Mr. Sinclair proposed a moment of silence in memory of Robert Brydone-Jack. Hawkins could not attended this ceremony because he had not yet returned from accompanying the body of Brydone-Jack back to Vancouver. The railroad builders were soon to experience more tragedy.

BENNETT
THE TRAIN COMES AT TWO

Weather was severe during the winter of 1898-9, with temperatures reaching 60 below. On February 24, four days after the summit ceremony, the upper pass was caught in a blinding snowstorm, trapping two locomotives and crews. Construction foreman Hugh Foy shoveled all night with a party of his men to free the trains. By morning he was exhausted and flushed with a high fever. He died early in the morning of February 28, the day he was scheduled to take his first vacation. The winter had claimed a second victim from among the supervising staff.

Since days were short and the weather severe, Heney favored a shorter work day with pay increased to 35 cents an hour. Hawkins was reluctant to increase wages because of decreased income. The railroad had relied on income from miners enroute to Atlin gold fields, but that traffic stopped in January when the government of British Columbia decided that Americans could no longer hold claims in the Atlin area.

The railroad management feared competition from the Chilkoot Pass aerial tramways. In order to increase railroad travel over the White Pass, they authorized Heney to establish the Red Line Transportation Company to carry supplies by horse and sleigh from Summit to Lake Bennett. Stikine Bill Robinson took charge of Red Line, recruiting all available packers and their animals. Heney agreed to provide this service to the railroad at cost, but found it difficult to keep up with the amount of freight arriving at Summit by train.

Some workers were disgruntled when the higher rate of pay was denied. Agitators announced a strike and, by March

2, 1200 men had left their jobs. Most of the citizens of Skagway supported the railroad, but some, like saloon keepers and aerial tramway operators, had ulterior motives and backed the strikers. After men had been striking for two weeks, some of the agitators threatened to burn down Camp 1. Hislop notified Heney of their threats, identifying Robert White as their ring leader. As the strikers approached the railway shops and roundhouse, Big Mike ran two locomotives onto the tracks with headlights pointing down the most likely path of attack. Heney, Dr. Whiting and Roadmaster Middaugh stood beside the locomotives, armed with Winchester rifles and wooden clubs. As 35 strikers emerged from the darkness, they were caught in the full glare of the train headlights. White ordered his men to stop and advanced alone drawing his revolver. Dr. Whiting moved out to meet White and struck him over the head with the butt of his Winchester. The rifle stock shattered and White slumped to the ground. The three men challenged the strikers to attack again. There was no move and the strikers vanished into the night just as the deputy marshal and his posse arrived.

The strike was actually a blessing for the railroad, since the weather was so bad that little could be accomplished. Without wages to pay, money could be saved. Hawkins decided to suspend new construction for the rest of the month and give the rotary snowplows a chance to concentrate on clearing the tracks. Heney decreased his work force to 300 men, but continued to deliver supplies to work sites in preparation for work in the spring. Fortunately Heney, whom Hawkins now referred to as "the contractor" could get the most out of his men. He directed, inspired, coaxed and demanded a level of performance beyond expectation from his unskilled crews. If he heard of a slowdown or reluctance to do a difficult job, Big Mike would motivate the men by tackling it himself. With responsibility for the Red Line Transportation Company in addition to railroad construction Heney accomplished more than was expected.

The railroad had to reach Bennett. Until it did earnings would be limited. The management needed more income to complete this part of the right-of-way. As the summer of 1899 approached, revenues increased. Hawkins, still fearing competition from the Chilkoot tramways, received permission to start negotiations to buy them and shut them down.

After a month without wages, some men had spent all their money and were willing to return to work for 30 cents an hour, but recruiting was difficult because men could not be assured of work beyond Bennett. During the winter months, Heney's gangs had drilled and blasted through rock that barred

Shoveling snow from the railroad grade. June 1899
Yukon Archives, Whitehorse

the way. By early June, they had completed all of the rock work between Fraser Lake and the outskirts of Bennett. When the warm summer sun melted the snow, they were able to resume work along Summit Lake.

On June 7, Hawkins sent telegrams to Heney and Hislop urging that the railroad reach Bennett by July 1, regardless of the quality of the work. Big Mike had already planned the final push. The supplies were on the ground and camps had been established. Heney suggested several bridges be eliminated and replaced with rock fills. By the middle of June, a rough grade was complete from six miles north of Summit to Bennett City, and men were shoveling snow from the summit grade. Trains were stopped temporarily and all available manpower left for the summit to help remove the last of the snow and distribute ties and rails along the right-of-way. On June 21, crews began laying track toward Bennett. Men worked night and day, ignoring the Sunday no-work rule. They paid little attention to the quality of the work; that could come later. Heney directed construction from dawn to dusk. He rode along the Summit-to-Bennett grade on horseback, hitched rides on supply wagons, traveled with work trains and waded through water to reach work sites ahead of the rails. If there was a problem, Big Mike was there, his high boots covered with mud and a cigar between his teeth.

During the final push to Bennett, Hawkins sent a telegram to Heney, inviting him to bid on the construction beyond Bennett as an independent contractor. This was what Heney had been waiting for ever since the meeting more than a year before in the St. James Hotel. Track was within three miles of Bennett on the third of July, when progress was halted by an unfinished bridge. By working through the night, the bridge gang finished it on the morning of July 4.

Early on the morning of July 6, a steamer landed at Bennett with 200 passengers. They saw a sign on the front of a tent saying "White Pass & Yukon R.R. Ticket Office." Many rushed in to buy tickets, but there was no railroad. The ticket agent assured them that the train would arrive at two sharp and kept on stamping tickets, counting money and weighing dust. The travelers could hear the ring of spike-mauls on steel rails in the distance. Many went out to watch the men work, and some even offered to help.

A passenger train left Skagway at eight in the morning with invited guests, including Mrs. E.C. Hawkins, who was going to drive the final spike. After traveling the length of Broadway, the train entered the coastal forest and started climbing At Inspiration Point, 17 miles north of Skagway, it passed beneath a row of mountain peaks. On the opposite side of the pass, countless waterfalls dropped gracefully into space, and there were occasional glimpses of the Skagway River rushing down its narrow gorge. After lunch at the summit, the passengers transferred to flat cars with wooden benches because the track was still too rough for passenger coaches. As they approached Bennett, the passengers watched gangs of sweating men feverishly laying the final 300 yards of track on the bare grade in front of them. Klondike miners and Bennett citizens lined both sides of the right-

Laying the last rails into Bennett. July 6, 1899
Yukon Archives, Whitehorse

of-way cheering the workers on. The railroad staff escorted the guests to Heney's commissary tent where they dined on oyster soup, deviled fowl, lamb cutlets, roast sirloin of beef and boiled leg of mutton with caper sauce. Desserts included meringue pudding, strawberry or lemon Jello, compotes of fruit, oranges, bananas, raisins and peaches, followed by tea, coffee, wine and spirits.

As the last spike was hammered home, three sternwheelers

blew their whistles, and Big Mike's powdermen shot off twenty-one earth-shaking dynamite explosions in rapid succession. The official guests returned to Heney's tent to toast the railway with a glass of iced champagne and prepare for the journey home. When the train pulled out of Bennett that afternoon it carried, in addition to the guests, the 200 outbound Klondikers with half a million dollars in gold dust. As the overloaded train passed the construction camps, workmen cheered and toasted the noisy Klondikers. Heney had

**As the last spike was hammered home
three sternwheelers blew their whistles.**
Yukon Archives, Whitehorse

broken his own rule regarding liquor in the camps and distributed thirty kegs of beer along the line.

The Red Line Transportation Company was still needed to provide transportation for men and supplies during the winter. The following disclaimer accompanied each ticket:

> This pass is not transferable, must be signed in ink or blood by the undersigned person who, thereby accepting it and using it, assumes all risk and damage to person and baggage. The holder must be ready to mush behind at the crack of the driver's whip.

35

Dewars Crown Scotch carried as side arms is subject to inspection, and may be tested by the officials of the road or their duly authorized representative.

No passenger allowed to make any remarks if the horses climb a tree and each one must retain his seat if the sled drops through the ice until the bottom of the lake in reached when all are expected to get out and walk ashore.

**First passenger train out of Bennett
carried $500,000 worth of gold dust.**
Yukon Archives, Whitehorse

If a passenger has but one lung he will have permission to inhale the fresh air to the capacity of said lung, no more will be allowed.

CARCROSS
THE GOLDEN SPIKE

Trains could now carry freight as far as Bennett, so Heney's Red Line Transportation Company had to convey tons of supplies by boat to Caribou Crossing at the north end of Lake Bennett to connect with wagons for the trip on to Whitehorse. Stikine Bill Robinson designed a barge that could carry 150 tons of freight. It was shaped like an oblong box, with projecting ends built to facilitate freight loading. When it was finished, Robinson inspected both ends and announced, "I think we'll make this end the stern." He chalked STERN in large letters on that end. The craft, with upright boilers and engines attached to three propellers, moved so fast that Robinson nicknamed it the *Torpedo Catcher*. On the maiden voyage, Stikine Bill had trouble with the steering. With all three propellers churning, the *Torpedo Catcher* spun around and kept turning while spectators on the bank struck up a popular song of the day, "Waltz Me Around Again, Willie."

With help from the Red Line Transportation Company, the White Pass and Yukon Railway could assure through transport from Skagway to Whitehorse. Brackett's Road was out of business. The railroad had succeeded in closing down the Chilkoot aerial tramways. The White Pass and Yukon, with a virtual monopoly, posted gross earnings of $200,000 in August 1899. The expense of running the trains that month was only $25,000.

The Close Brothers in London had not yet decided to extend the rails beyond Bennett, so Heney's main job was aligning and ballasting the twenty miles of track that had been hastily laid. William Brooks Close arrived in Skagway on August 20 to see the new railroad for himself. He was so impressed by the continuing prosperity of the Yukon that, on August 23, he authorized the 70-mile extension from Caribou Crossing to Whitehorse. Michael J. Heney, as contractor, was to finish this section of the railroad according to the specifications of the Pacific Contract Company, controlled by the railroad and managed by Hawkins. Since Close was reluctant to give approval for the difficult section along Lake Bennett until he had raised more money, construction would start at Caribou Crossing, now known as Carcross.

A filling where Lewes Lake was. September 1899
Yukon Archives, Whitehorse

Big Mike was ready when he received word on August 24 to start building. By early afternoon, 500 men and 100 teams of horses were at work pulling scrapers through the Watson Valley towards Whitehorse. The *Torpedo Catcher* delivered rails and other construction equipment to Caribou Crossing. By September 4, 30 miles of the Whitehorse extension survey was completed. Heney planned to complete the grade and lay fifteen more miles of track between Caribou Crossing and Lewes Lake before winter so that supplies could be brought to the head of construction by train. While cutting a four foot wide trench through a narrow sandy ridge at the southern end of the lake, construction crews inadvertently drained Lewes Lake and flooded the Watson River valley. A group of Indians, drying fish some miles away were terrified that the "earth was going down." Two days later, Lake Bennett was brown with mud for 15 miles south of Carcross. Big Mike would need two bridges to cross the canyon they had created.

Hawkins was surprised and concerned on October 20, 1899 when he received a telegram from London telling him to start building the 27-mile section along Lake Bennett. He did not expect such a quick response, and was not prepared for the additional work. This meant that Heney would have to work simultaneously on two sections - the Carcross to Whitehorse extension and the stretch along Lake Bennett. By mid-October, temperatures were below zero and Heney's work force of 600 men and 130 teams of horses had to contend with permafrost while preparing the grade north of Carcross. Red Line Transportation wagons were bringing piles and timbers for the bridges at Lewes Lake. Men were building a swing-bridge across the Nares River, using a pile driver that they had floated down Lake Bennett the previous summer.

Heavy snow further hampered the operation of the railroad during the winter of 1899-1900. Every morning the rotary snow-plows faced eight-to-twenty-foot drifts Avalanches brought down rocks and trees that damaged the revolving blades When the winter storms subsided, Heney's crews stepped up their work. Although building the railroad was Heney's responsibility now, the new contract arrangement didn't really change their working relations. Hawkins, Hislop and Heney continued to work as a team.

The *Torpedo Catcher* was beached for the winter, so Heney made Stikine Bill the grading foreman on the line north of Carcross. Work was fairly easy between Carcross and Whitehorse, requiring few rock cuts. Along Lake Bennett, however, Heney's rock men had to do a lot of blasting to clear the right-of-way. Progress was so good on the northern section that Heney announced he would complete the railroad from Carcross to Whitehorse Rapids by June 1, 1900. The goals that Big Mike strove hardest to attain were those that he set for himself.

On April 1, Heney was in Skagway. *The Daily Alaskan* reported that he had 750 men already employed and wanted to hire 2000 more, paying rock workers $5.30 a day, less a dollar for room and board. The two 150-ton barges, that his men were completing on the ice of Lake Bennett, would be available to transport the supplies since the water would soon be open. Heney hired "Snow King" Moriarty to supervise track laying on the Whitehorse extension. He wanted to complete that section as soon as possible because the movement of men and supplies was increasing and the warehouses were bulging with freight for the Yukon.

By May 10, Heney had finished the Lewes Lake bridges,

**Driving the spike at Whitehorse: front row, left
to right, Robinson, Heney, and Hislop. June 8, 1900**
Yukon Archives, Whitehorse

and Moriarty was laying tracks to Whitehorse at the rate of two miles each day. The Lake Bennett ice went out on May 23, allowing rails to be transported by barge. Heney had 500 men working on each of his fronts, but advertised he could use 1000 more. Men were leaving again to go to interior mines. On the morning of June 6, Stikine Bill's graders reached Whitehorse. Moriarty's track layer were only five miles behind. That evening the track was less than two and a half miles from Whitehorse and workers were invited to work as many hours as the could. On the afternoon of June 8, the first locomotive made its official appearance in Whitehorse. There was no banquet this time. That would have to wait until tracks from Bennett reached Carcross.

On June 9, the White Pass and Yukon Railway could truthfully advertise passage from Skagway to Whitehorse, although barges were still needed on Lake Bennett. Heney's remaining concern was the closing of he gap between Bennett and Caribou Crossing before the end of July. Stikine Bill Robinson and Snow King Moriarty were moved with their crews to the Bennett section with Robinson preparing the grade and Moriarty laying the rails. Big Mike was always on the move, traveling by horseback, steamboat and canoe. He pushed but never shoved while checking the work force and bolstering morale .

By the end of the first week in July, Robinson and his 1000 men had five miles of grade ready, and Moriarty's crews had finished spiking two and a half miles of rails. An intense rivalry developed between Moriarty and Robinson that came to a head when Moriarty accused Robinson of holding him back. Stikine Bill bet Moriarty a new set of clothes that track layers would never reach his graders. Their gangs learned of the bet and the race was on.

When tracks had reached a point eight miles south of Carcross on July 26, Heney informed Hawkins that he would be finished by late in the afternoon of July 29. Samuel Graves arrived in Skagway on July 25 to be present at the driving of the last spike. The railroad offered Whitehorse residents a free ride to Carcross on a special train to join in the celebration. Construction continued throughout the night of July 28. By early morning tracks were within two miles of Carcross. Fifty visitors arrived by steamship from Bennett and 50 more from Whitehorse on the special train. The track was nowhere in sight, although the ring of hammer on spike could be heard in the distance. Heney, a showman to the end, had saved the last half mile to show the visitors how fast his men could lay rails. Samuel Graves, on board the steamer *Australian*, could see the graders and track layers at work along the shore.

When the last spike had been driven, Heney's job was done. As Graves and Hawkins were preparing to leave, they were told that the boys were planning a farewell dinner for Heney. To keep Heney from bolting, the organizers led him to believe the dinner was to honor Graves, who wrote as follows:

We had a great dinner and Heney never smelt a

mouse - though he seemed to think it hardly the thing for me to take the chair at a dinner given in my honour. But the boys assured him it was no time for formality. When the dinner was over, Hislop got up and proposed Heney's health, saying that the boys who were so soon to part wished to mark their appreciation of his never failing kindness and courage through all the dangers and troubles of the past two years. Hislop made a magnificent speech (fancy the shy, silent Hislop). It was one of the finest tributes to the good qualities of an old and tried comrade that could be put into language. Poor Heney was horror stricken - and yet pleased beyond words. After the applause died down, he stood silent before attempting to reply but soon found his voice and words, and made a manly reply. Hawkins then got up and presented Heney with the gold watch and chain from the boys.

The Toast and Resolutions presented to Michael James Heney at that dinner aboard the sternwheeler *Australian* summarized the job he had done in building the White Pass and Yukon Railway.

THE TOAST

We have camped by mountain and river,
We have slept and told yarns together,
We have broken bread at his table
And roughed it in all sorts of weather.
So let us drink to our brother,
"Good luck and a life in clover,
Good health, and wealth and a loving wife,
And good rest when life is over."

THE RESOLUTIONS

That WHEREAS the time is a hand when the last spike is driven, the last barrrowful of ballast dumped and the great WHITE PASS & YUKON RAILWAY receives its last touches from the hands of its builder and contractor; and,

WHEREAS, this brings with it the time of farewells, and the

separation into other fields of hardy adventure, of those who have braved the avalanche and scaled the summit together, and have shared the dangers and hardships of these Arctic solitudes; Therefore be it RESOLVED, that we hereby set our hands to this testimonial of our high appreciation of the character and conduct of Contractor M.J. HENEY, the builder of the White Pass and Yukon Railways; whom we have ever found to be a manly man, a true friend and a cheerful comrade; and that we present him with this souvenir of our affection and esteem, in the belief that it will pleasantly recall many Alaska formed friendships that are eternal, when he goes to other climes to blast a way through the mighty barricades of Nature, and pass them with the steam whistle which echoes civilization and prosperous development, and also, when he has driven his last spike and retired to slippered ease and a contented contemplation of his worthy achievements ...

"HIS" WORK

Road begun at Skagway, Alaska	April 1898
Road reached Whitehorse, Y.T	June 8, 1900
Road completed along lake	July 29, 1900
Length P&A R&Nav. Co., Alaska	20.4 miles
Length B.C.Y.RR, British Columbia	30.9 miles
Length B.Y. RR, Yukon Territory	59.1 miles
Length overall	110.4 miles
Length overall in Airline miles	80.0 miles
Cubic Yards of material moved	1,431,600
Cubic Yards of snow shovelled	476,000
Average grade to Summit per mile	141 ft.
Maximum grade to Summit per mile	206 ft.
Highest Altitude reached	2940 ft.
Gauge of road	3 ft.
Maximum curvature 16 degree radius	3593 ft.
One tunnel, length	245 ft.
Snow Sheds, length	3157 ft.

Construction of the White Pass and Yukon Railway from Skagway to Whitehorse is estimated to have cost $10,000,000. The originally planned extension up the Yukon River was never built. The Company used sternwheelers, instead, to carry passengers and freight on to Dawson City. First class tickets from Skagway to Dawson cost passengers thirty dollars. A total of 35,000 men worked on the railroad between June 1, 1898 and October 1, 1900. The 35 deaths from all

White Pass Summit in winter.
Anchorage Museum of History and Art

causes, including sickness and accidents, was not considered excessive under the circumstances. No Asiatic labor was employed during the construction.

Heney had finished his work on the White Pass and Yukon. He sold his teams of horses and most of his equipment, and announced that "the men who worked on the railroad extension for me have either been discharged or taken under the

White Pass Summit in summer.
Anchorage Museum of History and Art

wing of the operative department." On September 1, 1900, *The Daily Alaskan* announced that "Mr. Heney is getting ready to show the world he knows how to rest as well as work."

SEATTLE
"A LIFE IN CLOVER"

Michael Heney was well prepared for "a life in clover." Work on the White Pass and Yukon had earned him a small fortune. Seattle Sand and Gravel, managed by his brother Patrick was prospering. He still had good health, but no loving wife. Heney never married. He returned to Seattle, where he retained a suite at the Rainier Grand Hotel. In the winter he also kept a base of operation at the Holland House in New York City, where he regularly met with major financiers of the day. He shaved off his dark beard, and discarded flannel shirts and whipcord pants. A white Stetson replaced the black slouch hat, worn in White Pass days. He was often seen driving a fine carriage and team of horses over the hills of Seattle.

Real estate investments in Seattle and San Francisco did well and his fortune increased. Dr. Fenton B. Whiting, who returned to a lucrative private practice in Seattle, described this phase of Heney's life as follows:

> During the long months and years which followed his first endeavors in Alaska, the "Pathfinder" once more mingled with the throng, and adapted himself to the conventionalities of civilization in the great cities of the outside world. A born aristocrat, he soon once more conformed to the customs and ethics of society. This came easily to men of his type, due to his normal innate instincts. As an astute, polished clubman, he was also a success, although disdaining the many frivolities of that, to him, artificial life,

45

where he seldom encountered real he-men of his type. As a pastime, however, it served temporarily as a substitute for something better. White collars and tuxedos meant nothing to him, although with his handsome, intellectual features and muscular, erect physique, he bore them well, and with a dignity commensurate with such paraphernalia. He presented a commanding and conspicuous figure midst gatherings of the social whirl.

During this period M.J. become known for his generosity, as Dr. Whiting points out:

But his greatest pleasure and pastime in this present idleness, was his wonderful philanthropy. It is more blessed to give than to receive was his motto, and these were his happiest moments, although he seldom made known his gifts, even to his closest friends. Heney gave for the pleasure of giving only, and his hundreds of voluntary donations will never be known. He shunned notoriety.

Heney kept in touch with his boys, who had worked with him on the White Pass. Although many of them were involved in other building projects around the world, they promised to be available should Heney undertake another railroad project. M.J. also kept in touch with the White Pass & Yukon management, taking a trip on the railroad each summer to see old friends. He watched the development of Alaska and the Yukon carefully. On June 22, 1901, *The Valdez News* reported:

Among the arrivals on the steamer *Bertha* last Wednesday morning was Mr. M.J. Heney, the railroad contractor and builder of the famous White Pass and Yukon railroad. Mr. Heney is accompanied by two civil engineers, Messrs. H. Harper and S. Murchison. The party brought with them six horses, camping outfits, etc., and will travel overland from Valdez to Eagle City, visiting the copper and placer districts and other points on the way.

The arrival of Mr. Heney and party caused considerable excitement in Valdez and visions of railroads floated before every one's eyes. When seen by a *New's* representative, Mr. Heney stated that the great expanse of territory between Valdez and Eagle had been talked of so much that he had a desire to investigate for himself and that was his mission now.

In regard to railroads, Mr. Heney said one would undoubtedly be built but just how soon he did not venture an opinion. However, Mr. Heney's reputation is to "work first and talk afterward" and the general opinion is that he is not on a strictly pleasure trip.

Heney and his party made the 400 mile trip from Valdez to Eagle City in thirty days. In early August, they arrived in Skagway on the White Pass and Yukon. Heney stayed several days in Skagway to handle affairs of his friend, John Hislop, who had died earlier that year in a train accident while in Chicago on his honeymoon. When questioned by reporters at points along the way, M.J. refused to comment on the purpose of the trip or his findings. On arrival back in Seattle, he surprised the hopeful Alaskans by giving a negative report. He was quoted in an August 14 interview with the *Post Intelligencer* as saying:

> So far as I can see, there is absolutely no excuse for promoters or capitalists interesting themselves in the construction of a railroad through that part of the country, or in other words from Valdez to Eagle City. If conditions were such as to warrant the construction of a railroad, it would have been done long ago, but it will be many years before a locomotive is seen in the Copper River valley.

Heney went on to state that the actual building of such a railroad would not be difficult because the soil was good and the grades not excessive. He estimated a railroad from Valdez to Eagle would cost about $12,000,000, but did not feel potential revenues would warrant the investment of private capital. He was evidently aware of the recent discoveries of copper ore in the Wrangell Mountains since he showed several copper bullets that he had acquired during the trip. In closing, Heney stated:

> Without a railroad this section of Alaska will never be developed, and until it is developed it will be difficult to get capital to invest in such an enterprise. If it was the Canadian government, they would probably render assistance of such a nature that the road could be built.

The Valdez News had a difficult time understanding Heney's negative report and commented on August 31: "It looks very much indeed as though Mr. Heney had a purpose in saying what he did in Seattle, but what that purpose is can only be guessed at. However there are other railroad builders in the world besides Heney and more than one of them have their eyes on the All-American' route." Rumors at that time suggested there had been a split among the financial backers of the White Pass and Yukon regarding the extension of that line, and that some of the backers were planning to invest in a competing line from Valdez to the Yukon. Some writers have since speculated that Heney may have been commissioned by the White Pass and Yukon Company to make a negative report in order to discourage potential competition. A more likely explanation is that he was acquiring background information so that he would be prepared to move when the time was right.

During the next two years, at least nine different groups announced plans to build railroads from Valdez to provide access to the copper deposits. The Burlington Railroad was ready to start in 1902, but postponed construction until the courts cleared title to the copper lands late in 1904. In the meantime, prospectors discovered coal and oil in the Bering River area east of the Copper River Delta. The Bering River coal rush was on, even though the United States did not have coal laws that could be applied to the unsurveyed land in the District of Alaska. A railroad would need coal to operate, so promoters began to think of Katalla, the new boom-town in the Bering River coal fields, as a possible port for a railroad. The proposed routes from Valdez did not provide access to any coal.

Heney was enjoying a holiday trip around the world in the summer of 1905. On the way back to the United States, he planned to spend a month in London. The day after arrival there he stopped in to see his friends at Close Brothers. One of the partners asked him whether he had heard about all the proposed railroads in the Copper River region of Alaska. Heney indicated that he had been out of contact with Alaska for several months. The banker then presented the following proposition to Heney, "You did such an outstanding and profitable job for us on the White Pass that if you know of a better route than the others, you can count on us for the financing."

Heney was bored with his "life of clover." Here was the chance he had been waiting for. Rising from his chair, he said, "Gentlemen, get one of your boys to go to some good bookstore and purchase for me the U.S. War Department Compilation of Exploration in Alaska. In the meantime I will go to the American Express Co. office and cancel all my reservations and have them make a reservation on the first passenger ship for New York." Then he stopped at the telegraph office and sent the following wire to Earl Siegley, his secretary and confidential advisor, "Tell all the boys we are going to get busy and that they are on the payroll as of today."

About ten days later he arrived in New York and wired Siegley to have his boys meet him at the Washington Hotel in Seattle. Archie W. Shiels, Heney's commissary manager, gave the following report of that meeting:

> He told us at dinner of his conversation with Close Bros., and said that he had spent all his time on the ship and on the train studying the narrative and the maps, that the report of Lieut. Swatka on his trip down the Copper intrigued him very much and convinced him that if a right-of-way could be found through Abercrombie Canyon, that the best route would be from Tidewater up through the Copper district to Abercrombie Canyon and thence to the

mines, a distance of some 200 miles. There were two big questions: could we bridge the Copper River between the Miles and Childs Glaciers, and could we find a right-of-way through the canyon. That, he added, was what Sam (Murchison), Jack (Dalton), and himself were going to find out. M.J. had caught a very bad cold while crossing from Liverpool to New York, and at this point Dr. Whiting, our chief medical man, threw a monkey wrench into the proceedings by saying, "M.J. you are of course my boss, but as your doctor I am your boss, and I will be damned if I will permit you to make the trip with that cold. If there is such a hurry about it Sam and Jack will have to go without you." At this point I begged for permission to go along, arguing that I knew that section of the country, but the boss said, "No, you will have to stay here and help Siegley."

Murchison, Dalton, J.L McPherson, a competent surveyor, and a cook left on the first boat to Valdez, where they picked up packers and pack horses. Heney instructed them to go from Valdez to Copper Center on the Government Trail, make their way to Chitna and then down the Copper River. On arrival at Orca (Tidewater) they should get a boat to Valdez and then plan to wire Heney in Seattle: "Meet me in Juneau" if the route was feasible, or "Will be home on the first boat" if not.

When M.J. recovered from his cold in about ten days, he was "champing at the bit" to hear from his men. Finally the favorable message came, and Heney caught the first boat to Juneau, arriving there before the others. He went immediately to the Land Office and asked if anyone had filed an application for a right-of-way up the Copper River and through Abercrombie Canyon. On being told that no one had done so, he replied that he wanted to do so right away. The Land Office accepted his verbal filing, providing maps followed within ten days.

Two days later, Murchison and his party arrived. They reported that the route was possible, but difficult, with enough room for only one right-of-way through the canyon. They believed that the bridge could be built if it was started right after breakup and completed before the ice went out the following year. The Murchison party provided the map to complete the filing.

Engineers, hired by the Eastern copper interests, had surveyed both the route from Valdez and the Copper River route earlier that year. Since they did not think the glaciers could be passed, they had not bothered to file the Copper River survey.

CORDOVA
A CITY IS BORN

$\mathbf{M}$.J. Heney had taken the first step towards building a railway up the Copper River. The crucial right-of-way through Abercrombie Canyon was his. M.J. and his boys were busy that winter making preparations for construction to begin. Sam Murchison reported on his return that there was an abandoned cannery near the native village of Eyak that had a large warehouse, a cook-house and a bunkhouse, all of them in good condition. M.J. sent Archie Shiels to San Francisco to purchase the abandoned cannery from Alaska Packers Association.

M.J. was convinced that the railroad should start at Eyak where there was an excellent sheltered harbor. Katalla was closer to the Bering River coal fields, but did not have a protected harbor and was subject to violent storms. While on trips to Alaska, Captain Johnny O'Brien had frequently told of the narrow escapes he had had trying to anchor there.

The most serious problem was funding. A railroad up the Copper River would be considerably more expensive to build than one from Valdez because much of the right-of-way would have to be on pilings and bridges. M.J. was willing to use his own fortune, and Close Brothers would commit an equal amount, but that would not be nearly enough to complete the railroad.

A source of additional funding appeared when Daniel Guggenheim announced in New York City that he was interested in building a railroad to the interior of Alaska and developing copper mines in the Wrangell Mountains. Heney hurried to New York with Samuel Graves, the representative of Close Brothers, to present his plan for a railroad. Dr. Whit-

ing gives an amusing account of how Heney summoned Stikine Bill Robinson to New York, and showed the massive hay-
seed from North Anson, Maine, the glories of the big city
while making plans for construction the following spring.

The Eastern capitalists did not endorse Heney's plan They
had already acquired the right-of-way for a railroad from Valdez through Keystone Canyon. With coal potentially available, they were also intrigued with plans to build from Katalla.
Heney decided to go ahead and build anyway with a million
dollars of his own money. Graves agreed that Close Brothers
would commit an equal amount on the assumption that Heney
could force others to buy them out to obtain the right-of-way
through Abercrombie Canyon. Both Heney and the English
owners of the White Pass and Yukon had filed claims in the

Driving the first spike on Copper River Railway. August 28, 1906
Cordova Historical Society, Cordova, Alaska

Bering River Coal Fields and wanted railroad access to their
claims. Since the Easterners were already making plans to
build a railroad to the Bering River coal fields, Heney would
get both a profit and access to the coal claims if he could sell
the right-of-way.

Heney was ready to gamble. On March 13, 1906, an advance
party arrived at Orca Bay and established a canvas camp four
miles down the beach. A telegram from Heney several days later
specified that the new town should be named "Cordova." On
his recent trip, Heney had been impressed by Cordova, Spain, a

beautiful city in a sunnier climate. On April Fool's Day, M.J. landed with a load of freight and snoose-chewing railway workers. The Copper River Railroad had arrived.

Cordova grew rapidly. The first issue of the *Cordova Daily Alaskan* announced that 500 men were working and had cleared five miles of roadbed. The first load of tracks arrived in July, and the first spike on the Copper River Railroad was celebrated on August 28, 1906. In September, "Old No. 50," the only locomotive actually purchased by Heney, arrived in Cordova.

M.J. Heney knew that he did not have enough money to build the railroad. His strategy was to force the Alaska Syn-

Heney's first gang on Copper River Railway.
Anchorage Museum of History and Art

dicate to provide the financing. All through the summer, he had crews drilling "coyote holes" in the walls of Abercrombie Canyon. The September, 1906 issue of *Alaska Monthly* announced:

> Occupying a narrow, rock-bound right of way on the western shore of the Copper River, the forces in the employment of M.J. Heney, builder of the White Pass & Yukon railway, have absolute control of the route for the projected new railroad from Cordova to the interior of Central Alaska, says the *Seattle Times.*

The vantage ground will not be surrendered to the forces of rival companies unless they can work through several dynamite-fortified stations, constructed under the direction of Mr. Heney. Should any rival contracting firm undertake to invade the territory occupied by Heney and his men, fatalities are certain to ensue.

Heney will use dynamite to fight any encroachment along the west side of the Copper River, which, engineers say, offers the only feasible route for a railroad up the stream. For a great distance the slender thread of the line will have to be blasted out of the solid rock. There is room for but one railway. Engineering facts make that certain.

Violence never erupted in Abercrombie Canyon, probably because everyone believed that Heney meant what he said.

In the meantime, the Copper River Railway faced another problem. Men were threatening to leave and go to Seward to work on the Alaska Central Railway. While Heney was in New York city attempting to raise money, Dr. Whiting worked out a unique solution to the problem. By rubbing Croton oil on the skin of one of his patients, he produced a rash resembling smallpox. As Health Officer, he then quarantined the town. No ships were willing to dock at Cordova to pick up the defecting men.

Dr. Whiting's ingenious scheme did not have long lasting benefits. The workers soon had to look elsewhere for work. Late in the fall of 1906, Heney told them that he had sold the Copper River Railroad to the Guggenheim-Morgan Syndicate for $250,000. M.J. had won his gamble, but he had not convinced the Alaska Syndicate to use Cordova as the port. Their engineer, M.K. Rogers planned to build a breakwater at Katalla that would make a safe harbor. The only part of the Copper River Railroad he planned to use was the right-of-way in Abercrombie Canyon. Heney was to retire, and Cordova was abandoned.

KATALLA
RAILS NEVER MEET THE SAILS

$\mathbf{M}$J. Heney returned to the social life of Seattle and New York City during the winter of 1906-1907. In the summer he took a long trip down the Yukon

Parts of river steamer *Chittyna* on Tasnuna Divide.
Anchorage Museum of History and Art

River, and visited the Bering Sea coast. His arrival in Nome started rumors that he was considering railroad construction there. When questioned by a reporter, Heney, replied: "There has been a lot of talk about a railroad to Siberia. I just wanted to take a look at the Bering Sea to make up my mind whether it should be bridged or dammed."

Back in the Copper River Delta, the Alaska Syndicate was concentrating efforts to link newly purchased copper mines with the coal fields. Although they still kept their Valdez right-of-way, their engineer M.K Rogers was building the breakwater at Katalla. The Syndicate managers located a flat area on the Copper River midway between Katalla and Cordova for the smelting plant to process Kennecott copper ore with Bering River coal. They purchased a steamship line and several locomotives. During the winter of 1907 they took apart the river boat *Chittyna* and arranged to have it packed in pieces across Marshall Pass from Valdez to the upper Copper River, so they could use it to supply camps along the right-of-way above Abercrombie Canyon. No expense was barred; but 1907 was to be a disastrous year for the Alaska Syndicate.

The stage was set in November 1906 when President Theodore Roosevelt temporarily withdrew all lands in Alaska from filing and entry under the coal land laws. *The Alaska Transcript* analyzed the situation as follows:

> If this cablegram means all it says, it is the hardest rap that Alaska has yet received for it will stop all the railroad building now going on to the westward. The government has not only refused to grant any assistance to railroad building in the way of subsidy, but it now removes the chief incentive that is prompting private capital to proceed further with their gigantic undertakings. Already millions of dollars have been invested in railroad surveying and construction. Scores of men have spent several of the best years of their lives in the development of one of Alaska's future chief industries, and now they are left "holding the sack" by this order to "withdraw from filing and entry" all coal lands.

The withdrawal of Alaska coal lands may have been motivated by eastern coal interests, though "trust busting" was also a priority for Roosevelt. Political columnists began to accuse the Guggenheim-Morgan coalition of attempting to create a monopoly in Alaska. Conservation was also a popular topic of the day. Roosevelt, influenced by his friend Gifford Pinchot, a New England millionaire with a passion for forests, added millions of acres to the National Forests which Pinchot directed.

In 1907 almost all of the nearly treeless land in the Bering River coal fields was placed in the Chugach National Forest, thus creating an additional layer of bureaucracy.

Reaching the copper mines was still a priority for the Alaska Syndicate, so construction on the railroad from Katalla continued throughout the summer of 1907. The Syndicate must have had some lingering doubts about Katalla as a port, because they retained Erastus C. Hawkins, Heney's former associate on the White Pass and Yukon, to resurvey all three possible railroad routes, the right-of-ways from Katalla and Valdez, and Heney's Copper River Railway from Cordova.

Valdez was again burning with railroad fever. Henry D. Reynolds, an unscrupulous developer, had persuaded some citizens of that town to invest money in his Alaska Home Railroad. Valdez residents, upset with the Guggenheim decision to build their railroad from Katalla, willingly joined Reynolds in an attempt to take over the right-of-way in Keystone Canyon. The Alaska Syndicate called upon Deputy Marshal Edward Hasey to protect their rock work. On September 27, 1907, the Reynolds men made an attempt to take the tunnel in Keystone Canyon by force. Hasey tried to discourage the 260 advancing men by firing in the air. When they failed to stop, he fired low into the crowd, wounding several men in the legs. Five days later, one of the men died from a wound infection. Marshal Hasey was indicted for murder. Newspapers and magazines throughout the country carried the story, and blamed the Guggenheim- Morgan Syndicate. The bad publicity continued through the trial because the Syndicate provided legal counsel for Hasey, and helped him get a light sentence.

The final blow came when fall storms hit Katalla and completely washed out the breakwater that M.K Rogers had built. E.C. Hawkins had, in the meantime, completed his surveys. Hawkins agreed with Heney's choice of Cordova for the railroad terminal. The Syndicate discharged Rogers and hired Hawkins as engineer. They called Heney out of retirement to finish the Copper River and Northwestern Railroad. His first contract called for completion of 50 miles of railroad to Abercrombie Landing by the end of the fall of 1908. Heney, as contractor, was responsible for laying the track, while the Katalla Corporation, under Hawkins' direction would build the three major bridges. Hawkins hired A.C. O'Neel as bridge engineer.

Storms continued to rage at Katalla. The one ship that managed to land there in November 1907, carried Hawkins and Heney on their first tour of inspection. The two surviving "Hs" were partners again in building a railroad in Alaska.

GLACIERS
THE "IRISH PRINCE" ENTERTAINS

The infusion of Guggen-heim-Morgan money allowed Michael J. Heney to build the railroad the way he wanted to. The Alaska Syndicate had already wasted millions of dollars in futile attempts to build from Valdez and Katalla; now they would at last get value for the dollar spent. M.J. picked up where he had left off a year before in Cordova. He had already laid four miles of track along Eyak Lake. His experienced crew was soon at work, because Heney had stipulated that his boys continue to be employed when he sold his Copper River Railway to the Syndicate.

Heney's first goal was the laying of tracks to Abercrombie Landing where trains could link up with river boats to carry supplies on up the right-of-way. Tracks would have to traverse miles of soggy tundra in the Copper River Delta and cross the Copper River twice to get there. While studying the Copper River route, Heney had discovered the secret to passing the Miles and Childs glaciers. Although the glaciers initially appeared to face each other across the Copper River, the Childs Glacier on the west side of the river was actually a small distance downstream from the larger Miles Glacier on the east bank. Therefore, if tracks crossed the Copper River below the glaciers, they could pass the Childs Glacier by running up the east side of the river. A second bridge would then be necessary to cross to the west side of the river again to pass Miles Glacier. M.J. used winter as an ally in crossing both the tundra and the river. By laying tracks on frozen ground and ice, he could transport his railroad supplies to

Abercrombie Landing, and also move tons of gravel from the glacial moraine to build a stable roadbed in the tundra of the Copper River Delta.

With the advent of spring, 3000 men were on the payroll. On July 4, 1908, the first train crossed the Copper River on a temporary trestle that ran parallel to the Flag Point bridge, which was being built by the Katalla Corporation. The *Cor-*

Railroad builders at Cordova, November 1908: from left, front row, James English, track superintendent; J.R. Van Cleve, master mechanic' Sam Murchison, construction superintendent; Michael J. Heney, contractor; Captain John J. O'Brien of Alaska Steamship Company; E.C. Hawkins, chief engineer; Alfred Williams, assistant chief engineer; (on step) Dr. F.B. Whiting, chief surgeon; P.J. O'Brian, bridges; back row, Dr. W.W Council, assistant surgeon; Archie Shiels, supply; Bill Simpson, steam shovel; "Stikine Bill" Robinson; and two unknowns.
Anchorage Museum of History and Art

dova Daily Alaskan referred to this event as "the crossing of the Rubicon," and remarked:

> M.J. Heney, the railroad builder, has crossed the Copper River with his iron horses and is now laying track on the island. Following up this island, for a distance of five miles, he makes another leap to the

other side of the river and from there hastens to the coal fields. It is the marvel of men familiar with railroad construction to note the progress being made by Heney and his bunch of hustlers. If someone doesn't head him off down at the coal fields, he'll scare old Juneau to death by running an engine into the place some time in the near future.

Actually the paper was not quite right in their assessment because all plans for completing the spur to Katalla had

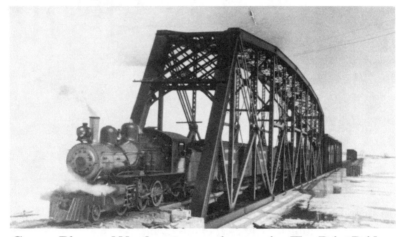

Copper River and Northwestern engine crossing Flag Point Bridge.
Anchorage Museum of History and Art

been suspended pending the reopening of the Bering River coal fields.

Heney completed his first contract by October 8, 1908, and stopped laying rails during the winter. Trains, crossing the Copper River on the ice, continued to move supplies for upriver construction camps to be ready for spring. A C. O'Neel, the engineer in charge of bridge construction for the Katalla Corporation also worked through the winter, observing ice conditions and making plans for the crucial Miles Glacier bridge. O'Neel hoped to begin sinking caissons through the ice in March to avoid icebergs and waves that were common in the summer.

On December 14, S.W. Eccles, President of the Copper River

and Northwestern announced the Alaska Syndicate's intention to extend the railroad to the Yukon River. Heney, returning to Seattle in January 1909 from a trip to New York, announced:

> The work of pushing the Copper River Railroad through to the Bonanza mines is assured. The question of money has been solved, for the Morgan and Guggenheim interest have pledged all the money, $12,000,000, that is necessary to put the line through.

Steamer *Nizina* unloading railroad construction materials.
Washington State Historical Society

> We will build the 150 miles to be constructed before November, 1910. That is the contract I made while I was back in New York.
>
> We are beginning the work now. That is, H.R. Simpson, assistant master mechanic, who came down to meet me, says the rotary snow plow is ready to be sent out on the line at any time. As soon as we complete our plans, which will be in about a month, we shall clear the present line and begin shipping our supplies to the end of the road. They will be freighted to the various points along the survey, where we will establish camps. In this way I shall be prepared to handle a large number of men as soon as the snow is off the ground. For the real summer work, the boats on the Copper River will be used to supply these camps, and by getting an early start, and having everything ready in the spring, I have no

hesitancy in saying that we shall have 50 miles of the road finished long before the snow flies.

The next 100 miles of the line can be rushed through easily, for during the coming summer the steamers will be used to carry supplies along the entire distance of the survey, so that when the following spring arrives, all we will have to do is to send our men to the various camps.

In regard to the question of whether the Copper River road will build a branch line to the Bering lake coal fields, I will say that no such move is contemplated until the government removes its restrictions

Main Street, Cordova, Alaska. 1908
Anchorage Museum of History and Art

on coal lands. There is nothing to induce a railroad to build there. The coal cannot be mined under the present conditions, for men cannot get patent to their holdings, and no one will sink money in property that has no title back of it.

The people I represent will build a road to these coal fields in a hurry if the laws will permit holders of coal lands to say they own them. This, however, is a matter that has been threshed out so often, it becomes irritating, rather than interesting. The government, not the railroad, is holding the country back.

Cordova thrived in the spring and summer of 1909. Every issue of the *Cordova Daily Alaskan* carried a description of the booming town, which boasted:

> Five grocery stores, five general merchandise stores, two lumber yards, two hotels, two hardware stores, three millinery and ladies' furnishing stores, four barber shops, four fruit and candy stores, two furniture establishments, five restaurants, one photograph gallery, one electric fixture store, two bakeries, one meat market, two paint and decorating stores, one upholsterer, two transfer barns, one sawmill with a capacity of 10,000 feet per day, six apartment houses, two drug stores, one blacksmith shop, one tailoring establishment, one bowling alley, two steam laundries, three hand laundries, five cigar stands, one bottling works, one stationery store and ten saloons.

Heney and Dr. Whiting with Governor Wilford Hoggatt.
Washington State Historical Society

Other accounts gave a more generous estimate of the number of saloons. The Episcopal church built a unique club house known as the Red Dragon. On weekdays the alter was hoisted by block and tackle to the ceiling. On Sundays it was lowered and chairs were set up for church services.

Heney supervised all aspects of the construction personally, as he had done while building the White Pass & Yukon. He lived in canvas tents at the construction sites, and cruised from camp to camp along the Copper River in his personal river boat, the *Little Willie*. M.J. took special delight in entertaining old friends and dignitaries in his hospitality tent. Dr. Whiting reports: "Alaska's governor dropped in, now and then, took off his official mask, and thoroughly enjoyed the 'Irish Prince's' well-known hospitality, with a very notable relish. Intimate old friends, they now sat and discussed present and past events in the making of Alaska." Attorney General Wickersham and Secretary of Labor Nagel, both members of President William Howard Taft's new cabinet, visited Cordova and enjoyed a ride up the railroad to the glaciers in a comfortable passenger coach. Major W.P. Richardson of the Alaska

Officers of the cableship *Burnside* meet with Copper River and Northwestern Railroad officials. August 21, 1908
Washington State Historical Society

Road Commission, visiting in June, stated his intention to run a road from the end of the railroad at Chitina to the Valdez-Fairbanks road as soon as tracks were laid. Episcopal Bishop Rowe visited frequently, as did magazine writers and professors from famous colleges. Author Rex Beach and his brother-in-law, actor Fred Stone, spent several months with Heney during the spring and summer of 1909, for the dual purpose of hunting bear and gathering material for a novel, *The Iron Trail*. Beach describes a meeting with M.J. Heney in his book, *Oh, Shoot!*:

It was hours before breakfast time when we arrived, but M.J. himself was at the dock, for a purser on one of his freight steamers had apparently mislaid a locomotive or a steam shovel or some such article which Mr. Heney wished to use that morning, and he had to come down and find it. He was not annoyed—it takes more than a lost, strayed or stolen locomotive to annoy a man who builds rail-

Heney playing with his pet bear cub.
Washington State Historical Society

roads for fun rather than for money and chooses a new country in which to do it because it offers unusual obstacles.

He welcomed us, drippingly, with a smile of Irish descent which no humidity nor stress of fortune could affect.

"Bear?" said Mr. Heney, "Yes, indeed. We'll see that you get all you want." And from that moment until we left Alaska with our legal limit of pelts he made us feel that the labors of his fifteen hundred men, the building of his railroad and the disbursement of millions of dollars were, as compared with our comfort and our enjoyment, affairs of secondary importance. And when we described to him the tints of our wall paper and rugs we got the impression that whether we needed bears lavender, bears mauve, or bears cerise, it was thenceforth a religion with him to see that we found them.

Heney, 4th from right, meets with officials of Alaska Syndicate.
Washington State Historical Society

In late July, Cordova was honored by a visit from the National Editorial Association. The *Cordova Daily Alaskan* wrote that about 40 or 50 of the editors were taken by train to the glaciers, where they were treated to a lunch that was reminiscent of feasts M.J. served to White Pass & Yukon guests:

Cream of Celery
Queen Olives   Mixed Pickles
Lobster Salad, with Mayonnaise
Fresh Halibut,   Breaded, Tartar Sauce
Prime Ribs of Beef, au Jus
Oyster Patties
Saute of Mushrooms, ala Maryland
Asparagus   Pecan Sauce

Corn on Cob   New Potatoes
Lemon Cream Pie   Assorted Cakes
Vanilla Ice Cream

After viewing the glaciers and Abercrombie Canyon, the party enjoyed sandwiches and all kinds of liquid refreshment while returning to Cordova. Later that year, H.C. Hotaling of Mapleton, Minnesota published a fifty page booklet with an account of the trip, which included this description of Heney:

> Just one glance at his face convinces one that he is a man who does things. He is of nervous temperament, quick and alert, and in order to accomplish what he undertakes stays with his men no matter how unpleasant or disagreeable the conditions. He is a royal entertainer... Thousands of miles distant from a source of supply, he served a banquet such as might be expected at Delmonico's.

Hotaling further commented that the railroad "opened to tourists a spot unexcelled in all the world."

By August 1909 residents of the Copper River country had good reason to hope that the Bering River coal fields might again be opened to entry. Theodore Roosevelt was no longer in the White House, and William Howard Taft had appointed Richard Ballinger, a former mayor of Seattle, secretary of the Interior. Ballinger had many Seattle friends and associates who had coal claims in Alaska, and he was committed to finding a resolution to their problems.

Early in August, Heney sailed for Seattle on business that may have related to development in the coal fields. Two weeks later a railroad right-of-way was filed for the Kush-Ta-Ka Railroad, which would serve the area where Heney, his brother Patrick, and the "English Group" had claims in the Bering River coal fields.

69

SHIPWRECK
THE BEGINNING OF THE END

$\mathbf{M}$.J. Heney sailed from Se-
attle the morning of August 24 on the steamship *Ohio* with a
load of railroad supplies and 35 horses that he probably
planned to use in the coal fields. M.J. never trusted the sea,
but his work in Alaska forced him to make many ocean trips.
The ship captains were special friends with whom he spent
many hours during these voyages. Shortly after midnight on
August 27, 1909, he was on the bridge of the *Ohio*, talking
with Captain John Johnson when they were interrupted by a
sharp jolt. The ship had hit an uncharted rock as it was enter-
ing Finlayson Channel in Canadian waters 450 miles north of
Seattle. Captain Johnson was aware immediately that the ship
was badly damaged but hoped to beach it before it sank.

Heney helped the crew wake the passengers up and get them
into lifeboats. Then he went below decks in an attempt to free
his horses so they could swim to shore. While he was with the
horses, power failed and the ship started to sink. When he managed to get back on deck all the lifeboats were gone.

Heney, along with Captain Johnson and several other men
who had remained on board, was forced to dive in and swim
half a mile to shore. M.J. was a good swimmer, but clothes
weighted him down. He was on the verge of sinking when a
lifeboat came along side. There was not enough room for
him in the boat but one of his friends held him by the collar
and towed him to shore. Four people drowned that night,
including the wireless operator, the purser and two passengers. None of the horses were saved.

In spite of his narrow escape, Heney took charge of the

situation when he reached the shore, as reported in a special dispatch to the *Cordova Daily Alaskan*:

> Through the generosity of M.J. Heney the passengers and crew were made comfortable at Swanson's Bay. He purchased all the available clothing in the place, bought pipes and tobacco for the male passengers, and is hailed by the passengers as the best of fellows. The people at Swanson Bay gave all the aid in their power. Heney is the heaviest loser out-

S.S. *Ohio* on the morning of August 28, 1909.
Courtesy of John Hellenthal

> side of the ship owners, but smiles in the face of all and praises the work of all the officers of the ship. Capt. Johnson piloted the boats through the shoal water to as near the beach as possible. Heney lost ties, rails, building material, and thirty-five head of horses. Much of the cargo will no doubt be saved, but delay means much to him.

Heney also took care of the dead. When the body of the wireless operator, George Eccles, washed ashore at Swanson Bay, Heney ordered a crude coffin to be made, secured ice from a fishing boat, and wired his agents in Seattle to spare no expense in finding the relatives and arranging for an undertaker to take charge of the remains upon reaching Seattle.

Approximately 225 people were on board the *Ohio* that night, many of them from Cordova. Some of the survivors

Heney (back row center) with survivors of *S.S. Ohio* shipwreck.
Courtesy of John Hellenthal, nephew of
Clarence Cunningham (identified by arrow)

continued north to Juneau on the *Humboldt* while others, including Heney, boarded the *Rupert City* and returned to Seattle. Upon arrival in Seattle, M.J. acted as spokesman for the survivors, assembling the group at the Rainier Grand Hotel to prepare testimonials to thank the Canadians at Swanson Bay and on the *Rupert City* for their help.

Heney had other matters to attend to in Seattle. He promptly bought more horses, which were scheduled to be shipped to Alaska in early September. A severe chest cold, from which he never completely recovered, delayed his own return to Cordova. Years of heavy smoking and exposure to rock dust had undoubtedly weakened his lungs and heart. When he did arrive in Cordova on September 18, the local Cordova band met him, playing "Hail to the Chief." He announced that he planned employ 3000 men and push work on the railroad forward with all possible vigor.

Heney thanked Cordovans for wanting to give a banquet in his honor, but requested that any celebration be deferred to a later date because he was anxious to "go out on the line" immediately. Heney "hated being made a fuss over," as Samuel Graves attested before the banquet in Heney's honor on completion of the White Pass and Yukon. M.J. praised the work his boys had done in his absence, by stating "they have done much better than if I had been here." He did attend a small dinner given by Dr. Whiting, at which he related the story of the sinking of the *Ohio*.

The following morning, Heney returned to the front, but, Dr. Whiting reported:

> Although escaping a watery grave in the wreck of the *Ohio*, Heney had not emerged unscathed. A changed Heney arrived at Cordova on a returning ship to the scene of his greatest activities. His arrival was the occasion of a joyous homecoming reception from citizens of all ranks. Children gathered about with childish greetings, most of whom had been recipients of his whole-hearted generosity. Alaska's biggest man was now once more back in his element, and departed the following morning for the front, where he was welcomed by his thousands of loyal workers. But the old fighting heart now failed to respond to an over-active brain; the lithe, muscular physique had lost that graceful swing so familiar to his old associates...

M.J. remained at the front, personally supervising the construction, until the last spike was driven at Tiekel River on November 30, 1909. The first 100 miles of the Copper River and Northwestern Railroad was completed. Cordovans were pleased because some of the traffic to the Interior could now go through Cordova rather than Valdez. Heney made one more trip to New York City to turn over the completed portion of the railroad in person to the Katalla Corporation. While returning to Seattle, he became seriously ill and was forced to spend the next two months at Paso Robles Springs in California.

While M.J. was attempting to regain his health, the Ballinger-Pinchot Controversy raged over claims in the Bering River coal fields. *Collier's Weekly* ran feature stories

and editorials excusing Interior Secretary Ballinger of being in collusion with the "Guggenmorgan" or "Morganheim" monsters. In Washington D.C. a Congressional Committee was investigating both the Interior Department and the National Forest Service. When James Wickersham, Alaska's new congressional delegate, jumped in on the side of the conservationists, Heney commented publicly on the controversy that must have caused him much distress during his final illness.

Alaska delegate to congress, James Wickersham. *Alaska State Library*

Wickersham's accusation that Major W.P. Richardson of the Alaska Road Commission was lobbying for the Guggenheim and Morgan interests prompted M.J. to state in a January interview with the *Seattle Times*:

> James Wickersham is a political sorehead. Any man he can't use he wants to put in the gutter and walk on him.

Wickersham is the political maverick of Alaska and any man he can't use he wants to ruin. Richardson has done more for Alaska than any other living man and every white man in the North stands behind him...

The Alaska delegate thinks that the Guggenheims and the Morgans are the worst people in the world, but he didn't think so until he applied to Steven Birch, one of the heaviest stockholders of the Bonanza mine, for the support of those interests and their endorsement of his campaign, and it was re-

**Construction camp at Mile 125 Copper River
and Northwestern Railroad. July 1910**
Anchorage Museum of History and Art

fused him. Since that time the Guggenheims are fiends incarnate and must driven from the earth, according to Wickersham.

In the same interview Heney commented on Wickersham's efforts to attain Home Rule for Alaska:

What Alaska doesn't want is politics. The country is full of nation savers who can't go out and earn their three meals a day, and if they don't have to talk politics they could get out and dig a little and help themselves and the country.

The greater part of Alaska's population is not permanent, being composed of men who go there to make the money and then get out. Under these conditions the country has no license to ask for a territorial form of government.

Heney kept in touch with his workers back in Cordova. At the start of the new year he wired Archie Shiels: "Please convey to the boys my sincere appreciation of a splendid service during 1909 and my best wishes for their welfare in the new year." Later in January the *Cordova Daily Alaskan* announced:

Million Dollar Bridge under construction.
Anchorage Museum of History and Art

Through the generosity of Contractor M.J. Heney, Cordova is to have a full fledged brass band. When Mr. Heney returned from the states last fall, he was approached on the subject of the organization of a band, and at that time stated that if the boys would get together and let him know just what they wanted he would purchase the instruments for them.

Mr. Shiels left last night for Puget Sound and immediately upon his arrival there he will place an order for a good repertoire of music and the follow-

ing instruments with the Johnson Musical Company:
E flat tuba, euphonium, two valve tenor trombones,
three harmony horns, two B flat clarinets, an E flat
clarinet, two cornets, drums and cymbals.

M.J. was physically unable to return to Alaska in the spring
as he had planned. Dr. Whiting arrived in April with the news
that Contractor Heney had recovered from a recent severe
attack of the grippe and would return to Cordova in June. He
further commented that Heney was enjoying a hunting and
fishing expedition in California and developing into an ex-
pert angler while attempting to regain strength for the strenu-
ous season ahead.

The much hoped for recovery did not occur. Heney was
not present in May 1910 when the crucial span of the Million
Dollar Bridge was successfully bolted in place moments before the ice went out of the Copper River, carrying the sup-
porting falsework with it. Although Heney devised the plan
for crossing the river between the glaciers, A.C. O'Neel and
E.C. Hawkins deserve the credit for building the Million Dollar Bridge.

While confined to bed in a San Francisco apartment, M.J.
kept in close touch with Alaska politics. On August 5, 1910 the
Cordova Daily Alaskan printed the following telegram from
Heney in bold face type across the front page of the paper:

> The best interests of Alaska, and particularly Cor-
> dova, on account of the early opening of the coal
> fields, demand the election of Orr, who will be in
> harmony with the administration in Washington.
>
> Wickersham is wholly discredited, and if elected
> could accomplish nothing, as he has, by his false
> representations, antagonized the administration
> and all of Alaska's best friends. For the honor of
> Cordova I hope its citizens will most emphati-
> cally turn him down. He has, by every conceiv-
> able falsehood, done his utmost to injure the
> enterprises and interests which are making Cor-
> dova the metropolis of Alaska. I hope my friends
> will vote for Orr.

In a September letter to Dr. Whiting, M.J. still expressed hope of recovering enough "to navigate under my own steam." On October 11, 1910, a week before his 46th birthday, Michael James Heney died of pulmonary tuberculosis, complicated by pneumothorax and myocarditis.

Construction camp flag flies at half mast on hearing of Heney's death. October 11, 1910
Washington State Historical Society

KENNECOTT
THE COPPER SPIKE

Both Cordova and Seattle mourned Heney. Editorials and articles reviewed his life and praised his character. These words, spoken at the memorial service in Cordova by Judge John Goodell, are typical of the eulogies:

> In saying a word in honor of the memory of Mr. Heney, the first thing that comes to mind is the intense loyalty given him by all the men who worked with him and for him and under him. I have never heard any one of these men speak a word against him. He had more than their total support: he had their respect, their admiration and their love. In this respect he differed from any other great and successful man I have known. To find the reason for this we have only to look at the character of the man, his bigness of heart, his ready sympathy and his exact sense of justice. No actor is so great that he can pretend these things. Instinctively, all who knew Mr. Heney felt them, and so in fair weather and foul weather, in adversity or in prosperity, they were his men, and proud of the title, "One of Heney's men."
> Mr. Heney had not only indomitable energy and courage, and wonderful executive ability, but he had also combined with them in a remarkable measure, the prophetic eye, the soul of the poet and the dreamer. It was given to him to look on the waste places of the earth, and see them in his mind made

glad with prosperity. It was given to him to gaze at a bay like this, rock-ribbed and desolate, and see on its inhospitable shores a city, to see its waters teeming with the commerce of the world, and there was also given to him the energy and courage to go about the bringing of these dreams true.

Heney's generosity was again evident when the details of his will were made known. He left an estate of over a million dollars. Bequests, either in the form of lump sum payments

Sam Murchison and E.C. Hawkins
driving the copper spike. March 29, 1911
Washington State Historical Society

or lifelong annuities, were made to relatives and associates, including Captain Johnny O'Brien. Other generous sums were left to Catholic charities and to Episcopal Bishop Rowe to benefit Alaskan Indians. An editorial in the November 1910 issue of *Alaska-Yukon Magazine* commented that "only a few intimates among the beneficiaries themselves know what the bequests meant in sympathetic understanding of unspoken needs, in tactful recognition of tender sensibilities and little frailties, and in unselfish desire to be secretly kind rather than openly generous."

Over 1000 friends and business associates attended funeral services for Heney at the Catholic Cathedral in Seattle. His brother Patrick Augustus Heney erected a monument to his memory in the Calvary Cemetery where he is buried. The National Board of Geographic Names honored M.J. by naming the range of mountains overlooking Cordova, the Heney Mountains. The highest point is called Heney Peak. Beyond the Million Dollar Bridge, the railroad right-of-way passes across the moraine of Heney Glacier.

After Heney's death, work on the Copper River and Northwestern was pushed through under the direction of E.C. Hawkins, with Sam Murchison acting as contractor. The railroad was completed to the Bonanza mines on March 29, 1911. During the Copper Spike Ceremony, the first engine, Old No. 50, stood by, puffing and whistling, with a large portrait of the late M.J. Heney over the headlight.

The standard gauge Copper River and Northwestern, mockingly called the "Can't Run and Never Will" extended 196 miles from Cordova to the Kennecott copper mines. The total cost of construction was $23,500,000, all private capital. Although the projected extension to the Tanana river valley was never built, the railroad reimbursed its investors richly. In May 1915, a single train carried $345,050 worth of copper ore. During 1916 alone, the railroad carried $32,000,000 in high grade ore. In addition, the Copper River and Northwestern route became one of the prime tourist attractions in Alaska until operation ceased in 1938. Thousands of visitors to Alaska marveled at the Miles and Childs glaciers and the snowcapped peaks of the Wrangell Mountains. One of the most popular scenic tours of that period was the Golden Belt Tour with tourists leaving their ships either at Cordova or Seward. Those arriving at Cordova took the railroad to Chitina, continued by car to Fairbanks, and returned to Seward on the Alaska Railroad.

THE IRON TRAIL
REX BEACH TELLS THE STORY

$\mathbf{M}$ichael James Heney was a doer, not a writer. He did not keep a diary, and few of his letters have been preserved. His own words, when quoted in newspapers, were terse and factual. On occasion they revealed his sense of humor. Samuel Graves, the president of the White Pass and Yukon, has given us word pictures of Big Mike as he lived and worked while building that railroad. Popular novelist Rex Beach provides in his novel, *The Iron Trail* some true-to-life descriptions of M.J. during construction of the Copper River and Northwestern. Shortly after the first installment of that novel appeared in the January 1913 issue of *Everybody's* magazine, the editor of the *Cordova Daily Alaskan* commented: "Those who know the local situation can readily recognize in the leading character, Murray O'Neil, the well remembered and splendid characteristics of the late M.J. Heney."

Murray O'Neil is Heney in every respect, even though Beach has changed the sequence of events and created a fictional love affair for popular tastes. The heroine, Eliza Appelton, may represent Rex Beach himself, for Beach, like Eliza, was a magazine writer with an interest in conservation.

In the spring and summer of 1909, Beach spent several months with Heney while the latter was building the Copper River and Northwestern. Years later in his autobiography, *Personal Glimpses*, Beach revealed that this was more than a hunting trip:

> I explained that I hoped to do a novel based on
> the exploits of Michael J. Heney, a railroad builder

whom I had met the year before. Mr. Heney, known in the Northwest as "the Irish Prince" had built the White Pass & Yukon, a spectacular piece of railroad construction; now he was in a race to lay rails to the rich mineral region near the upper reaches of the Copper River. It involved almost insurmountable engineering and construction difficulties, he was meeting with stiff competition, there had been strikes, riots and bloody conflicts over rights of way, all of which made me feel sure that a lively story was unfolding and that I was the man to write it. It was a story that would deal with the newly adopted policy of conservation as well as with the spectacular doings of a daring operator.

Rex Beach, like Eliza Appelton, may have been a trust-busting conservationist when he came to Cordova. He had earlier been responsible for exposing a fraud in Nome that was the subject of his novel *The Spoilers*. Whatever his original intent, his experience that summer made him a lifelong admirer of Michael Heney. In 1931 he wrote in the forward to Dr. Whiting's book *Grit, Grief and Gold*:

We are accustomed to think of trappers and fur traders, the miners and farmers who blazed the trails in the West and North, as pioneers. They broke new paths of destiny, to be sure, but, they were merely scouts and explorers, the real pioneers were the rail builders. Those sturdy fellows who drove tunnels and built bridges and laid steel were the true empire builders, for, with every mile of grade thrown down, they thrust the frontier back a corresponding distance. It was they who brought comfort and security and made life on the edge of things worth living.

No country offers more difficulties and discouragements to the "rail pioneer" than Alaska. In addition to the obstacles encountered elsewhere, there are others which can be conquered only by the exercise of courage, resourcefulness, fortitude and perseverance.

M.J. Heney, affectionately known to his friends and

admirers as the Irish Prince, was a brave, resourceful, and determined man. He was a great railroad builder, too, and his success was a tribute as much to his knack of handling men and inspiring loyalty, as to his engineering genius. My admiration for him and my interest in his accomplishments prompted me to write a fiction story based upon one of his Alaskan undertakings.

Heney was photographed on several occasions during the construction of the Copper River and Northwestern, but none of those photos picture the man as well as Rex Beach does when describing Natalie's meeting with his hero after the sinking of the *Nebraska*:

> Murray O'Neil had recovered sufficiently to go among them with the same warm smile which had made him friends from the first. In the depths of his cool gray eyes was a sparkle which showed his unquenchable Celtic spirit, and before long smiles answered his smile, jokes rose to meet his pleasantries ...
>
> For her part she beheld a man of perhaps forty, of commanding height and heavy build. He was gray about the temples; his eyes were gray, too, and rather small, but they were extremely animated and kindly, and a myriad of little lines were penciled about their corners. These were evidently marks of expression, not of age, and although the rugged face itself was not handsome, it had a degree of character that compelled her interest. His clothes were good, and, in spite of their recent hard usage, they still lent him the appearance of a man habitually well dressed.

During the months that Rex Beach spent hunting in Cordova and observing the railroad construction, Heney must have spoken of his dreams for the development of Alaska. Beach has recorded them in his description of Murray O'Neil as he first conceives his plan for bridging the Salmon River between the glaciers:

The world owes all great achievements to dreamers, for men who lack vivid imagination are incapable of conceiving big enterprises. No matter how practical the thing accomplished, it requires this faculty, no less than a poem or a picture. Every bridge, every skyscraper, every mechanical invention, every great work which man has wrought in steel and stone, and concrete, was once a dream.

O'Neil had no small measure of the imaginative power that makes great leaders, great inventors, great builders. He was capable of tremendous enthusiasm; his tem-

Heney (right) enjoying a lunch break with Track Superintendent, James English.
Courtesy of Peggy Gaudetle, grandniece of M.J. Heney

perament forever led him to dare what others feared to undertake. And here he glimpsed a tremendous opportunity. The traffic of a budding nation was waiting to be seized. To him who gained control of Alaskan transportation would come the domination of her resources.

In *The Iron Trail*, the reader often feels that Rex Beach may be using the actual words of Michael J. Heney when Murray O'Neil speaks. In describing his own role during the railroad building, Murray O'Neil says, "Oh, I'm like Marcelline, the clown at the Hippodrome - always pretending to help, but forever keeping underfoot. When it becomes necessary I raise the money to keep the performance going."

When the breakwater at Kyak (Katella) washes out in a storm, Murray O'Neil tells Eliza of his triumph:

"I saw it in a dream ... I saw a deserted fishing village become a thriving city. I saw the glaciers part to let pass a great traffic in men and merchandise. I saw the unpeopled north grow into a land of homes, of farms, of mining camps, where people lived and bred children. I heard the mountain passes echo to steam whistles and the whir of flying wheels. It was a wonderful vision that I saw, but my eyes were true. They called me a fool, and it took the sea and the hurricane to show them I was right."

In the words of Murray O'Neil, as he explains his position to Eliza, we can see the frustration that Heney must have felt over the closure of the Bering coal fields.

"Conservation is no more than economy," he declared, "and no one opposes that. It's the misapplication of the principle that has retarded Alaska and ruined so many of us. The situation would be laughable if it weren't so tragic." ...

"Our ancestors blamed King George for their troubles more than a hundred years ago and a war resulted. But every abuse they suffered is suffered by the people of Alaska today, and a lot more besides. Certainly England never violated her contracts with the colonies half so flagrantly as our Government has violated its contracts with us. ...

"This country needs two things to make it prosper — transportation and fuel. We are doing our best to supply the first in spite of hindrance from Washington; but the fuel has been locked away from us as if behind stone walls. Rich men must be brave to risk their dollars here under existing conditions, for they are not permitted to utilize the mines, the timber, or the waterpower, except upon absurd and unreasonable terms. Why, I've seen timber lying four layers deep and rotting where it lies. The Government won't save it, nor will it allow us to do so. That's been its policy throughout. It is strangling industry and dedicating Alaska to eternal solitude. Railroads are the keys by which this realm can be unlocked; coal is the strength by which those keys can be turned. The keys are fitted to the lock, but our fingers are paralyzed. For eight years Alaska's greatest wealth has lain exposed to view, but the Government has posted the warning, 'Hands off! Some one among you is a crook!' Meanwhile the law has been suspended, the country has stagnated, men have left dispirited or broken, towns have been abandoned. The cost in dollars to me, for instance, has been tremendous. I'm laying my track alongside rich coal-fields, but if I picked up a chunk from my own claim to throw at a chipmunk I'd become a lawbreaker. I import from Canada the fuel to drive my locomotives past my own coal-beds which I have paid for — and I pay five times the value of the fuel, forty per cent of which is duty. I haul it two thousand miles, while there are a billion tons of better quality beneath my feet. Do you call that conservation? I call it waste."

The Iron Trail is dated, but still well worth reading for vivid descriptions of the Copper River Delta, exciting accounts of dynamiting Abercrombie Canyon, and building the Million Dollar Bridge. The use of fictional names for people and places is confusing at times, as is the altered sequence of events. The reader should be aware that Rex Beach fabricated a happy ending. The real ending is bittersweet at best.

EPILOGUE
"CAN'T RUN AND NEVER WILL"

When Heney died in October 1910, the future looked bright for his railroads. The White Pass and Yukon was flourishing. The Copper River and Northwestern was nearing completion, the main obstacles conquered. William Howard Taft was more receptive to resource development than Roosevelt had been. Interior Secretary Ballinger was at least trying to resolve the stalemate in the Bering River coal fields. Coal might soon be available to process copper ore in Alaska. The Copper River and Northwestern Railroad might be able to use the local fuel.

The bubble of optimism soon burst. Within a week of Heney's death, the *Cordova Daily Alaskan* announced the indictment of numerous coal claimants, including the late M.J. Heney. These indictments asserted that the claims were fraudulent because the locators never intended to develop the coal lands for themselves alone, as stipulated under the Coal Law of 1904. Court cases dragged on for years until all of the original claims had been cancelled on technicalities. The claimants spent thousands trying to prove up, but never even got back their filing fees. By the time the federal government developed regulations for leasing coal lands, no one was interested. They didn't trust the government any more.

Although the Congressional committee investigating the Pinchot-Ballinger controversy decided in favor of Ballinger, Pinchot succeeded in so inflaming public opinion that Ballinger resigned in 1911. He was succeeded by Walter L. Fisher, an ardent conservationist. Articles in *Collier's Weekly* and other newspapers and magazines continued to accuse the Alaska

Syndicate of trying to control all of Alaska's resources. Cartoons showed monsters, labeled "Guggenmorgen" and "Morganheim" invading Alaska. James Wickersham, Alaska's congressional delegate, continued to denounce the Alaska Syndicate, greatly exaggerating its potential power and misrepresenting its motives.

Cartoon published during Pinchot-Ballinger controversy in 1910.
Washington State Historical Society—Curtis Collection

The Conservationists persuaded Theodore Roosevelt to run for president in 1912 as a third party candidate, so splitting the Republican party that Woodrow Wilson won election in

1912. As a final act of his presidency, William Howard Taft created the Alaska Railroad Commission. After studying possible routes to the interior of Alaska, the commission recommended both extending the Copper River and Northwestern and building a railroad from Seward to Fairbanks. They gave top priority to the Copper River extension, estimating that a railroad from Chitina to the Tanana Valley would cost $13,000,000. The Alaska Syndicate offered to sell the Copper River and Northwestern to the federal government for

Cordova coal party. May 4, 1911 *Alaska State Library*

less than their $23,000,000 construction cost. The Wilson administration, fearing adverse public opinion if they made any deal with the hated Guggenheims, declined the offer. Three years later the federal government built the Alaska Railroad from Seward to Fairbanks at a cost to the taxpayers of over $70,000,000.

If they could have used Bering River coal, the Guggenheims might have extended the Copper River and Northwestern at no cost to the taxpayers. However, they were adamant that they would not spend more on the railroad unless the government changed its policy on coal claims. Cordova citizens, incensed at having to import Canadian coal, staged the Cordova Coal Party, dumping a boatload of imported coal into the bay. The Copper River and Northwestern converted its engines to burn oil. The

Syndicate directed its efforts towards mining high-grade copper ore at the Kennecott mine. A smelting industry never developed in Alaska. The high-grade ore went to Tacoma for processing, and Guggenheim money left Alaska with the copper ore. Further extraction of lower grade ore was not cost effective due to the expense of shipping it out of Alaska. The Kennecott Copper Corporation closed the Kennecott mines in 1938, and abruptly stopped running all trains. They sold the tracks for salvage and gave the right-of-way to the government. Cordova, once a bustling railroad town, reverted to being a quiet fishing village without land access to the rest of Alaska. The lingering hope that someday a highway would follow the path of "the Iron Trail" vanished in 1964 when a violent earthquake damaged the pilings of the Million Dollar Bridge.

A writer predicted in a 1910 issue of *Alaska-Yukon Magazine* that, by 1940, Alaska would be the fastest growing state with over three million people, and that Cordova would be the center of a smelting industry with "newspapers to rival San Francisco and Seattle." Harvey O'Conner, writing a book on the Guggenheims in 1937, noted that, instead, there were "deserted towns, rusted rails, ores hauled out of Alaska for processing, Asiatic labor manning the canneries, forests and coal fields untouched, people with no power, and a Government railroad lacking initiative or energy to bring tourists and settlers into the land."

A similar fate threatened the White Pass and Yukon. Tracks needed maintenance and rolling stock needed replacement when World War II started in 1941. The United States Army took over operation of the plucky narrow gauge to support the construction of the Alcan highway. After the war, tourist trade flourished on the White Pass and Yukon. Many visitors entered or left Alaska and the Yukon via the historic "trail of '98," with home-cooked meals in the mess hall at Lake Bennett. Paddle-wheel steamers carried tourists down the Yukon River and up the beautiful headwater lakes until 1955. The mainstay of the White Pass and Yukon, however, was the profit realized from transporting ore from interior mines to the coast. The highway between Whitehorse and Skagway opened in 1980 and took away the mining business. Tourist trade alone could not support the railroad.

The narrow gauge White Pass and Yukon is still intact. On May 15, 1988, trains again began to run 20 miles to the White Pass summit for summer tourists. Railroad owners negotiated with Canadian officials to extend the run beyond the Canadian border the following year. Trains run to Lake Bennett in the summer to accommodate Chilkoot Trail hikers. Weekly steam trains run to Bennett for tourists. Trains do not run as far as Whitehorse, but travelers can transfer to motor coach at Fraser to complete the trip. Thousands of cruise ship tourists make the round trip to Summit twice daily during summer.

Work train on the Copper River Northwestern Railroad.
Anchorage Museum of History and Art

Little remains of the standard gauge Copper River and Northwestern, the much acclaimed All-Alaska route of the early 20th century. The Copper River highway runs along the old railroad right-of-way as far as the Million Dollar Bridge at Mile 49, but conservationists blocked repair of the bridge.

A permanent bridge now crosses the Copper River at Chitna and the Kuskulana Bridge between Chitina and McCarthy has been repaired. A gravel road covers the old railroad bed to the Kennicott River, and a foot bridge provides access to McCarthy and the Kennecott mine buildings which are now part of the Wrangell St. Elias National Park. A decaying railroad trestle and flat tires resulting from buried spikes still remind travelers that this used to be a railroad. The Swiss-type resort hotels, predicted by Rex Beach, won't be there for the tourists, but campers can enjoy the canyons and glaciers along the lower Copper River while travelling by raft.

The railroad "can't run and never will", as its nickname predicted, but Alaskans of the 21st century may yet marvel at what M.J. and his boys did with pick and shovel 100 years ago.

Michael James Heney created two miracles during the twelve

River steamer in Woods Canyon.
Anchorage Museum of History and Art

years he worked in Alaska. He is quoted as having said, "Give me enough dynamite and snoose and I'll build a road to Hell!" We can only speculate on what might have happened had this Irish Canadian farm boy lived even twelve years more.

BIBLIOGRAPHY

Beach, Rex E.
The Iron Trail. A.L. Burt Co., New York, 1913.
Oh. Shoot! P.F. Collier & Son Co., New York, 1921.
Personal Exposures. Harper & Bros., New York, 1940.

Clifford, Howard.
Rails North. Superior Pub. Co., Seattle, 1981.

Graves, Samuel H.
On the White Pass Payroll. Lakeside Press, Chicago, 1908.

Herron, Edward A.
Alaska's Railroad Builder Mike Heney. Julius Lessner, Inc., New York, 1960.

Janson, Lone E.
The Copper Spike. Alaska Northwest Publishing, Anchorage, 1975.

Minter, Roy.
The White Pass. Gateway to the Klondike, University of Alaska Press, Fairbanks, 1987.

O'Conner, Harvey.
The Guggenheims, Covier-Friede, New York, 1937.

Shiels, Archibald.
The Kennecott Story, Privately published, Bellingham, Wash., 1964.

Warman, Cy.
"Building a Railroad into the Klondike." *McClure Magazine*, March 1900, pp. 419-426.

Whiting, Fenton B.
Grit Grief and Gold. Peacock Publishing Co., Seattle, 1933.

Wilson, Katherine.
Copper Tints. A Book of Cordova Sketches. Daily Times Press, Cordova, 1923.

The following newspapers and periodicals were also reviewed:
   The Alaska Monthly. Juneau, May 1906 - Nov. 1907.
   Alaska Sportsman. Seattle, October *1965.*
   Alaska-Yukon Magazine. Seattle, April 1905- July 1912.
   The Alaskan. Sitka, July 10, 1897.
   Collier's Weekly. New York, Sept. 18, 1909 - May 6, 1911.
   Cordova Daily Alaskan. Cordova, Jan. 21, 1909 - Apr. 1, 1911.
   The Daily Alaskan. Skagway, July 30, 1898 - Aug. 3, 1901.
   Ketchikan Miner. Ketchikan, Sept. 1, 1909.
   The Seattle Post-Intelligencer Aug. 14, 1901, Aug. 28, 1909.
   Oct. 12, 1910.
   The Seattle Times. Seattle, Oct. 14, 1910.
   The Valdez News. Valdez, June 22, 1901 - Aug. 24, 1901.

Index

95